Theology Today

Jürgen Moltmann

Theology Today

*Two contributions towards making
theology present*

SCM PRESS
London

TRINITY PRESS INTERNATIONAL
Philadelphia

Translated by John Bowden from the German
Was ist heute Theologie?,
Quaestiones Disputatae 114, first published 1988
by Herder Verlag, Freiburg, Basel and Vienna.

First published 1988
Second impression 1989

SCM Press   Trinity Press International
26–30 Tottenham Road   3725 Chestnut Street
London N1 4BZ   Philadelphia. Pa. 19104

British Library Cataloguing in Publication Data

Moltmann, Jürgen
  Theology Today—(Was ist heute theologie?)
  1. Christian theology. History.
  I. Title II. Was ist heute Theologie?
  230-09

  ISBN 0-334-02359-9

Library of Congress Cataloging-in-Publication Data

Moltmann, Jürgen.
    (Was ist heute Theologie? English)
    Theology Today: two contributions towards making theology
present/Jürgen Moltmann.
    p. cm.
    Translation of: Was ist heute Theologie?
    Contents: The presence of theology—The course of theology in
the twentieth century—Mediating theology today.
    ISBN 0-334-02359-9
    1. Theology. Doctrinal—History—20th century. I. Title.
BT28.m6513 1989
230'.09'04—dc20   89-5022

Phototypeset by Input Typesetting Ltd
and printed in Great Britain by
Richard Clay Ltd, Bungay, Suffolk

Contents

Preface

The Presence of Theology

In 1984 and 1986 I was invited to write two long articles for the *Enciclopedia del Novecento*, published by the Istituto della Enciclopedia Italiana in Rome. One was on 'Theology in the Twentieth Century' and the other on 'Mediating Theology' today. Because this comprehensive *Encyclopedia of the Twentieth Century* is appearing only in Italian and not in German, I am grateful to Herder Verlag and the editors of the series Quaestiones Disputatae for the possibility of publishing it in the original German. I am also particularly grateful to Heinrich Fries for his critical reading of the typescript. In order to keep the basic character of the first article, I have dispensed with detailed references and added a bibliography, which is arranged in order of the topics discussed. It can be taken as a reading list for further study. The second article goes more into detail, so it has notes and references.

Of course, this is not a history of theology in the twentieth century. I could not aim at completeness, and many people will look in vain for names which are important to them. Colleagues will wonder why they are not mentioned. I hope these limitations will be noted, and that the reader will concentrate on what I *have* said, rather than on what I have not.

The task I saw myself faced with was primarily to give a comprehensive account of theology in the present, its tasks, problems and most important trends. The perspective is my own, i.e. that of one who is affected by and involved in theology. I have not attempted to give a purely objective description, because even that would simply be a subjective intervention into an activity which is still in flux, disguised in the form of cool detachment. Nor have I attempted to practise self-denial. Any present-day theologian talking about theology in the present always speaks in a subjective and committed way. He or she cannot do otherwise. I am very well aware of these limitations of my own theological position.

On the other hand, precisely for this reason I have also become more profoundly aware of the need to make theology present and the difficulties of doing so – something with which all theologians have to struggle, but particularly those of modern times. Theology which is present is not just a theology of the present day in a chronological sense. Theology which is present must also be present in a kairological sense. To be present is a constant task of Christian theology which is never fulfilled in history. It is in a particular way a task of Christian theology, since this theology is the reflection of a historical, not a mystical faith. Because it speaks of God for Christ's sake, like Jewish theology it is directed towards historical recollection and the testimony which hands that recollection on. It must 'make present' the fundamental historical recollection of Christ, in order to interpret the present in the light of that and to open up the future which is being headed for in that historical past. As long as historical faith can disclose the future to the present in historical recollection it is a living faith, and its theological reflection is relevant. Once that is no longer possible, the historic recollection of Christ fades into the distance of past history, and the theological orientation of the present passes into other hands. To make present the historic recollection of Christ and the tradition of his gospel is thus a vitally important task of Christian theology.

That is what Pope John XXIII thought when at the opening of the Second Vatican Council he used the term *aggiornamento* as a watchword. The word does not just mean adaptation, modernization and making up for lost time; in essence it means 'making present'. Of course the adaptation of the tradition to new forms of present consciousness and present culture is part of this 'making present'. How can theology make itself understandable to its contemporaries unless it translates tradition into the language of the present? Adaptation should not lead to disintegration; rather, the substance of the gospel only becomes recognizable in the process of translating the tradition into the present. Only as the outer garments of theology change between the Middle Ages and modern times, and between modern times and what may be a 'post-modern' age, does one recognize who is wearing the garments and cease to confuse the wearer with one set of garments or another.

The way in which acts of violence and unjust suffering contradict and oppose the cause of Christ which has been handed down to us is also part of this 'making present'. Saving faith always has a therapeutic task as well as the hermeneutical task of the theology of historical faith. Making theology present cannot just be a matter of adaptation to the spirit of modern times; it must also be participation in the sufferings of this time and resistance to those who cause them. The saving and liberating potential of the historical recollection of Christ is not just manifested in 'modernism'; it first becomes evident through participation in the history of suffering in the present, by taking the side of the victims of the 'modern world'.

'Presence' is not least a gift; it is not just a task of Christian theology. Anyone who is 'present' is where he or she is expected. Anyone who has 'presence of mind' thinks of the right word, to bind or to loose, at the right time. He or she does what is necessary in the given situation. In this sense 'presence' does not just mean this year or next, but the kairos which is given today and only today. A theology which discovers its 'presence' in this sense is truly present theology. No theologian has this dimension of being 'present' under control. No one can produce it. But every theologian can seek it and be open to the right time. Any theologian can perceive and interpret the signs of the times. Any theologian can detect the suffering of this time and take part in it, in so doing becoming a 'contemporary'.

'The presence of theology' means more than 'making theology present', however much it presupposes the making present of theology in the hermeneutic process of tradition and reformation and in the therapeutic process of adaptation and resistance.

The 'presence of theology' also means more than 'making theology present', in that every theology which sets out to be present is concerned, and must be concerned, with this presence. Theology which is present and the ways in which theology is made present aim at achieving this 'presence of theology' in the divine kairos of the time. I hope that these two small contributions will indicate this, for that is what I had in mind.

Tübingen, 31 January 1988   Jürgen Moltmann

I

The Course of Theology in the Twentieth Century

1. The nineteenth-century legacy

World history cannot be divided by centuries. It has its own course and its particular periods. By 'nineteenth century' here I mean that period of European history which began in 1789 with the French Revolution and ended in 1917/1918 with the First World War and the Russian Revolution. This is the world which emerged from the bourgeois revolution and which was shaken to its foundations by the socialist revolution. The bourgeois world constantly sought to interpret itself, in order to legitimate itself. It was essentially concerned to explain itself. I shall begin by taking the two most important but mutually contradictory interpretations as illustrations of the contradictions left behind by the nineteenth century and the most important problems of Christian theology in the twentieth century: the 'vision of freedom' and 'the authoritarian principle'. Theology is always related to the situation of the church. In modern times this is in turn conditioned by the social, cultural and political situation. So we must begin with this situation of the world in the nineteenth century, in order to

1

understand the shape of the church and the way in which theological theory has been formed.

First, the vision of freedom. 'Freedom, equality, brotherhood' were the principles with which the French Revolution began. They are the ideological foundation of the bourgeois world. The old European society of 'estates', which was both clerical and feudal, was shattered. A new egalitarian society was constructed, one based on achievement. What determined the value of a human person was not birth, but achievement. The sovereignty of the ruler and absolutist rule 'by the grace of God' was replaced by the sovereignty of the people, the authoritarian state was replaced by the democratic state, and subjects were replaced by free citizens. The states with a single confessional belief were done away with by the secularization of church property in 1803, and were replaced by states which were confessionally neutral, and in principle secular. In this way religion ceased to be a matter of state and became a 'private concern', a matter of personal decisions. The bourgeois called for freedom of religion over against the power of the state and freedom of conscience over against the authority of the church.

The build-up of the bourgeois world went hand in hand with the build-up of the industrial world. The new machines made the first 'industrial revolution' possible. This revolution brought about an enormous shift among the population of Europe: the masses streamed into the cities from the country-side, giving rise to great industrial conurbations, first in England and then on the continent. For the first time in history, all men and women could be treated equally – as a work-force and as consumers. Nationality, religion, culture, gender, race and anything else that made up human identity faded into the background in the face of these new egalitarian determinations. The move towards a bourgeois and industrial world burst open

2

the old class order and the historical limits of the old European world.

In principle the basic notions of freedom and equality are universal. They therefore had to be applied critically in constantly new ways where they were only being realized partially. When the bourgeois were established and formed a new ruling class, the proletariat whom they exploited took up these ideas and called for economic freedom as well as political freedom. The 'social question' was the great problem for European states in the nineteenth century. When the bourgeois of Europe set out on the economic colonization of the world, the oppressed colonial peoples had to take up these ideas and embark on the fight for freedom from European imperialism. The liberation of slaves and the abolition of the slave system in the USA and the European colonies were the great theme of the first half of the nineteenth century. The ideas of freedom and equality eventually and inevitably also spread to women who had been deprived of their rights by patriarchal culture, and inspired their emancipation movements.

The nineteenth century can rightly be seen as the period of struggles for freedom and revolts which aimed to realize the hopes of the American and French revolutions. The vision of the kingdom of freedom, justice and lasting peace for all liberated a tremendous potential of human energies in constantly new strata of the people and in increasing numbers of populations on earth. History was no longer endured passively as a destiny or providence. For the first time human beings became aware of their power, raised themselves up to become subjects of their history and took over responsibility for their future. Here a far-reaching change in modern mentality is evident: life is no longer orientated on what is derived from tradition; instead it is orientated on the future through hope and planning. Personal and social life is no longer ordered in harmony with the eternal laws of the cosmos on the basis of

3

natural law; rather, reality is experienced as history, in the possibilities of which human hopes can be realized. Progress in the awareness of human freedom fully matched the recognition of the openness of the reality of human life and the natural cosmos to the future. The meaning of history was no longer sought in the past made present by traditions, or in eternity made present by religion, but in the open invitation of the future. The great leading ideas of the nineteenth century associate all hope with history and history with the future: revolution, evolution, emancipation, progress, growth, expansion. Even the modern division of history into three epochs – antiquity, the Middle Ages and modern times – shows the secularized spirit of messianism (Joachim di Fiore) in this world. As Friedrich Schlegel rightly declared at the beginning of this era: 'The revolutionary wish to realize the kingdom of God is the elastic point of all progressive education and the beginning of modern history.' But his interpretation of the modern world was only one side of things.

On the other side we find the authoritarian principle 'God, king and fatherland'. This is the expression of conservative reaction. It interpreted the phenomena of the modern world which I have just mentioned in contrary fashion as signs of a crisis in social order and the apocalyptic downfall of the world. The major European churches and their theologians consistently chose this conservative option in the nineteenth century. The Catholic philosophers De Maistre, Bonald and Donoso Cortes developed the state philosophy of counter-revolution, and later Rome also spoke in these terms. The German Lutheran theologians Julius Friedrich Stahl and August Vilmar described religion and church as the deliverance of the nations from the 'sickness of revolution'. The Calvinist theologian and Prime Minister of the Netherlands, Abraham Kuyper, commended 'reformation against revolution': all revolutions are directed against God. Democracy, the sover-

4

eignty of the people, liberalism and secularization are the diabolical names of the 'beast from the abyss' and signs of the outreach of chaos. Revolution against the ruling powers is rebellion against God, as is shown by the revolutionary cry 'Ni Dieu ni maître'. Therefore revolution leads to atheism and atheism to anarchy. Only religion can rescue the authority of the state. Only the authority of the state can keep the life of society in order. Only the churches can cure the peoples of the disease of revolution. Christian theism was presented as a religion supportive of the state, in that it provides transcendental legitimation for the unity and the hierarchical ordering of society. However, the apocalyptic age began with revolution and atheism, with liberalism and immorality, with democracy and human self-deification: it is the final bloody battle between Catholicism and godless socialism (Cortes); the last fight between Christ and Antichrist (Vilmar, Stahl); the irreconcilable opposition between the man of God and godless man (Kuyper). Since the French Revolution, and even more since the failure of the bourgeois revolution in 1848, the major churches therefore supported the conservative powers of order and flew an alternative conservative tricolor: 'God, king, fatherland' or 'God, family, fatherland'. They shaped themselves into the political power of the counter-revolution. The development of democracy in politics; of liberalism and socialism in the economy; of scientific technological rationality and the sense of freedom in culture therefore always came up against resistance from the churches and theology. In fact there is hardly any development of the modern spirit which did not initially come up against the resistance of the churches and theology. Only when the bourgeois age was reaching its end did churches and theologians hesitantly find positive attitudes to the developments of the modern world. Nevertheless, one cannot help noting that the basic anti-revolutionary, conservative option has determined the historical form of Christian

5

religion, the way in which it is given form in the church and presented in theology, down to the present day. The transforming process of the revision of this conservative basic option only began in the middle of the twentieth century and can hardly be said so far to have been successful.

The nineteenth-century legacy. The bourgeois world of the nineteenth century has come to an end in three ways. In the First World War the two Protestant-bourgeois great powers, Great Britain and Prussia-Germany, destroyed each other. The secular-bourgeois great power, France, was also destroyed. The Bolshevik October Revolution in Russia in 1917 meant for the bourgeois world precisely what that world had itself meant in 1789 for the feudal world of old Europe: the destruction of all its values and principles. Therefore the anti-Communist reaction among the bourgeoisie appropriated all the ideological elements of its former feudalistic enemies and now transferred them to 'Communism'. The basic anti-bourgeois option of the churches turned into a basic anti-Communist option. The outcome of the Second World War in 1945 then brought the end of Europe's rule over the world. The two super-powers of the USA and the USSR arose out of the ruins of Europe. European impotence also led to the liberation of the peoples of Africa, Asia and Latin America from colonial rule and imperialism. From now on the future of world history will no longer be determined just by Europe.

The tasks for the twentieth century arise out of the nineteenth-century legacy. So we can define this legacy in a series of contradictions, which have to be resolved if humankind is to survive.

1. The liberation of the economy from religion, morality and politics led to liberalism and thence to the development of capitalism. The conflict between capital and work led to the growth of the proletariat in the nineteenth century and

increasing unemployment on all sides from the middle of the twentieth. Scientific-technological developments benefit capital. The growing power of the multinational concerns removes them from national control and keeps trade unions from participation in shaping them. This development does not further the life of the mass of people if it is not brought under human control.

2. Scientific and technological civilization has led to a tremendous enrichment of life, but at the same time also to a tremendous increase in the numbers of humankind. The human race will have quadrupled between the year 1926 and the year 2020, from two to eight billion people. Overpopulation has become our fate. It has also involved nature and humankind in an ecological disaster from which no way out can yet be seen. But unless we overcome the ecological crisis we shall not survive.

3. The political forms of democracy which were developed in the bourgeois world of the nineteenth century evidently cannot spread further in the twentieth and have become insecure even in European countries. On the one hand, if human rights are to be implemented, there is no alternative to democracy. On the other hand, it is increasingly difficult to get a consensus of citizens on basic political questions. Therefore the old democratic forms of life are being repressed by the construction of modern bureaucracies and authoritarian controls. Military dictatorships are coming into being everywhere, in both the Western and the Eastern world. It is hard to ward off authoritarian modes of government even in old democracies.

4. Finally, while the nineteenth century left behind a European rationality which spread all over the world, it did not leave behind a politically united and powerful Europe. For that to be achieved, a Europe which has become particularistic needs to be relativized and integrated into a world culture

which is still coming into being, the form of which no one can yet foretell.

2. The starting-point of theology in the twentieth century

We cannot begin on the assumption that all groups and institutions in a society live synchronously in the same time. Progress is always made in a one-sided way. That is why there are so many anachronisms in modern societies. Religious ideas and ethical modes of conduct prove particularly resistant to the change needed to adapt them to new situations and their challenges. The organizations of the church and the forms of its life have an amazing staying power. The modern world often requires religion to be even more changeless than earlier cultures did: religious stability is evidently meant to make up for the instabilities of modern life. For that reason the internal problems of theology, too, are often not the contemporary problems of the society in which it is practised. There is a significant time-lag between the churches' existence and the life of the modern world. Therefore over large areas theology in the twentieth century is still preoccupied with the problems of churches and Christians in adapting themselves to developments in the nineteenth century, and still has to see clearly the new problems of the twentieth.

One can see a shift of phase even within the churches: the theological problems of the bourgeois world, scientific civilization and urban secularization were first taken up and worked through by Protestant theology; about fifty years ago they were hesitantly also taken up by Catholic theology; and only now is Orthodox theology coming to them. The Protestant theology known as 'liberal theology' was open to the bourgeois spirit as early as the beginning of the nineteenth century: freedom of belief, freedom of conscience and freedom of

8

association are the presuppositions for the freedom of theology itself. In the wake of Immanuel Kant this trend developed ethical theology; in the wake of Friedrich Schleiermacher it developed the theology of faith. Common to both is the new bond between faith, which is limited to the religious determination of personal existence, and scientific reason, which has been set free on all sides, so that faith does not get in the way of reason and reason does not dissolve faith. In this way a series of conflicts with 'modernism' were avoided, of the kind that shook Catholic theology to the depths. But even this peace treaty between Christian faith and scientific reason in liberal Protestantism was valid only as long as the bourgeois world could be regarded as a 'Christian world'. This form of the *Corpus Christianum* also fell apart in the horrors of the World Wars and the terrors of Fascist dictatorships.

The present situation of church and theology is dominated by the acute disintegration of the *Corpus Christianum* in its various historical forms. With the fall of the Christian Tsars in Russia in 1917 the Orthodox Church lost its last political support. That was the end of the Byzantine theocracy with which Orthodox theology had been bound up since Constantine the Great. The Roman Catholic Church set out on the process of detaching itself from the Catholic state of its own accord, in the Second Vatican Council held between 1962 and 1965. Its process of renewal was dominated by Pope John XXIII's slogan of *'aggiornamento'*. In the Protestant Church in Germany, during the Church Struggle against Hitler between 1933 and 1945 the 'Confessing Church' stood on its own feet. The other European state churches and national churches also learned attitudes of resistance to the power of the state and turned into free churches, without formally becoming Free Churches everywhere. All three Christian confessions experienced the disintegration of the Christian states which had been shaped by them and prepared themselves to accept a secularized and pluralistic world.

Christians are learning to live in an indifferent, post-Christian and non-Christian environment. The churches are learning to exist in their own strength without political privileges. Christian theology is learning to make itself understandable without the presuppositions of a universal 'natural theology' which can be taken for granted. This process of disintegration can lead to the marginalizing of faith, the church and theology, or to ecumenism on a universal scale. It can lead to faith, the church and theology becoming insignificant, or it can lead to their becoming Christian. Therefore the new opportunities for Christianity in the twentieth century can also be put positively, as follows: faith as Christian faith, and no longer as European religion, in world-wide conversation with other religions and world-views; the church as the ecumenical church of Christ, and no longer as the bourgeois religion of Europe; theology open to the world for the testimony of the gospel in the coming culture of all humankind. The secularization of the old *Corpus Christianum* has given the church and theology the positive opportunity of becoming truly secular, namely open to the world and world-wide. The process of the de-Europeanizing and the universalizing of the Christian church and theology dominate the twentieth century.

3. In search of secular relevance

As long as the Christian church was at home in a Christian world, it lived in the environs of a world which it dominated and permeated with its spirit, a matching world. In this 'Christian world' Christian theology could presuppose a 'natural theology' to which all human beings assented on the basis of the 'sound human understanding'. 'Natural theology' was the term used to describe a universal and direct knowledge

10

of God: anyone can know in the light of natural reason that there is a God and that God is one. While Christian theology is based on the revelation of God as it is attested in Holy Scripture, in the *Corpus Christianum* it presupposes this natural theology as a preliminary stage of the knowledge of revelation or as preparation for it. In this way there came into being in the Middle Ages the great syntheses of Christian theology and natural theology, the *sacra doctrina* and the *prima philosophia*. The *Metaphysics* of Aristotle as they were communicated through Thomas Aquinas were regarded as the self-evident formulation of natural knowledge of God. Conversely, as a result of the synthesis with the natural theology of the *prima philosophia* Christian theology became the queen of the sciences and thus universal.

Since the beginning of the Renaissance the sciences have emancipated themselves from the limitations and the laws of this theological metaphysics. They have constructed their own world of scientific and technological civilization. In the modern scientific university theology is no more 'queen' than the church in the modern world represents the 'crown of society'. But if the world of the sciences is no longer compatible with a cosmos of knowledge the criterion of which is a metaphysical theology, then theology loses not only its pre-eminence but also its relevance. The modern general theories with which the sciences and their results are continually interpreted are post-Aristotelian theories and to the present day have a completely atheological character. They do not put in question the inner nature of theology, but its universal competence and relevance. They make theology in its traditional form functionless. How can theology make the universal claim of the one God generally comprehensible if it can no longer presuppose a universal, direct knowledge of God?

What function does Christian theology have in the world of the sciences, which have emancipated themselves from its guidance? So what form must Christian theology take in a secularized, post-Christian world, if it is to show its Christian determination and at the same time its theological universality? These problems used to be discussed under the headings of 'fundamental theology' in Catholic theology and 'apologetics' in Protestant theology. But the crisis has affected not only the external aspect of Christian theology but also its innermost being. So we find not only external adaptations of theology to the spirit of modernity but also serious attempts to sketch out a completely new form of Christian theology. They are all in search of the roles and functions in which Christian theology can become relevant in the contemporary situation and competent in modern questions. The whole of Christian theology is sketched out afresh, depending on the particular analysis of the socio-political and cultural-spiritual situation of the present. This procedure has also been called the *contextual method*: the text of theology to be communicated must be related to the particular context in which theology is situated. Here I shall introduce only the most important trends: 1. hermeneutical theology; 2. the theology of secularization; 3. the theology of liberation, going on in 4. to sum up the basic ideas of Christian theology in modern times.

1. *The critical consciousness and the demythologizing of Christianity*

The world-view of the New Testament is a mythical one; it speaks of heaven and earth and hell. History is a scene of supernatural powers, of God, the angels and Satan with his demons. Human beings are not free but controlled either by demons or by God. The description of the saving event matches this mythical world-view and is in mythological language: the Son of God comes down to earth from heaven, sacrifices his life on the cross, is raised from the dead on the third day, now

12

rules from heaven and will one day come for the Day of Judgment. For modern men and women, who have achieved a rational relationship to the world and to history, this mythical world-view is obsolete. Therefore Christian proclamation does not get to them if it is put in this traditional mythological language. Anyone who during the week accepts the validity of the laws of nature in the context of technology cannot religiously believe in supernatural miracles on Sunday. But is the Christian proclamation bound to the mythical view of the world? Does belief in Christ also call for the acknowledgment of this mythical world-view? Because this cannot be the case, Christian proclamation must free itself from the mythical world-view in order to be able to address men and women in the modern, rational world in a non-mythological language.

Rudolf Bultmann called this task the programme of 'demythologizing'. With it he accomplished the task of historical-critical research into the Bible and outlined the basic ideas of 'existentialist interpretation' which are still enriching the hermeneutics of the Christian tradition. The mythical world-view of the Bible was replaced by the scientific world-view of the nineteenth century. The feeling of dependence on supernatural powers was overcome by the sense of freedom among modern men and women. But what is the content of the Christian proclamation and to whom is it addressed? The Christian message bears witness to the faith which men and women have found through Christ. It is not addressed to their understanding of the world but to their understanding of themselves. Even in those mythical pictures of the world in the Bible people were predominantly interpreting themselves. Myth is already an expression of a self-understanding of faith, not a quest for an objective world-view. It is the task of a critical exegesis of the text to bring out the existentialist significance of statements of faith in their mythical modes of expression, in order to present these to men and women of today as a

13

possibility for their self-understanding. Human beings have to interpret and understand themselves. The basic human question is whether one understands oneself in terms of the world and one's own works, or in terms of God and faith. Christian proclamation is addressed only to this question of human decision. Therefore it can dispense with a unitary, religious world-view and detach itself from the world-views of past eras and of European cultures: our questions about ourselves and the truth of our humanity are untouched by this, since it is that question which makes human beings human.

Bultmann's concentration of demythologizing on anthropological interpretation was and is disputed. Even those theologians who shared his presuppositions did not accept all his conclusions. Can human self-understanding and human world-view really be separated? Can we understand ourselves without at the same time understanding our world? Does not existentialist interpretation lead into the constrictions of bourgeois private existence? Discussions on the hermeneutics of basic religious and cultural traditions after Bultmann have opened up wider horizons.

Hans-Georg Gadamer and Paul Ricoeur developed a philosophical hermeneutics of traditions in cultural change in which a variety of horizons to understanding and interpreting life merge and re-form. Not only our understanding of ourselves but also our world-view is part of a history of the extension and deepening of hermeneutics; there has been as it were a fundamental paradigm-shift on the basis of new insights, of the kind that we can see in the development of physics from Euclid via Newton to Einstein. Bultmann wrongly made the scientific world-view of the nineteenth century an absolute. We find the hermeneutical processes of the interpretation, application and revision of particular traditions in all spheres of life. It is therefore meaningful to regard an understanding of the world and human self-understanding as a unity and to subject this differentiated unity to that process of revision which is necessary if we are to respond to the challenge of the future in the present. That also applies to Christian proclamation, which cannot be limited to the soul or human existence, since it affects not only men and women but also their world and the cosmos, since God is the 'all-controlling power'.

The existentialist interpretation of the Christian proclamation was expanded on the other side by its political interpretation. The starting-point of political hermeneutics and sociological exegesis is that the mythical world-view of the Bible not only expresses the way in which people of that time understood the world and themselves, but also reflects social conflict and political struggles for power. The biblical traditions clearly show how the prophetic promise and the gospel of God conflicts with 'political religion'. All traditions of the Old Testament begin with Israel's exodus from slavery in Egypt. They are rooted in the experience of religious and political liberation and constantly made present in the feast of the Passover. All traditions of the New Testament are rooted in the resurrection by God of the Christ who was crucified by the Romans as a rebel. They are messages of a liberation which is really experienced and eschatologically hoped-for. Therefore even today Christian proclamation intervenes in the real, political world in a critical and liberating way and may not be limited to the 'private concern' of the pious citizen. Social and political hermeneutics sees the Christian church as a catalyst for the liberation of men and women from the limitations and constrictions of the 'bourgeois religion' of the modern world. It understands the Bible as a 'subversive', 'revolutionary' book in this world of inhuman violence and powers remote from God.

15

2. The secular world and the theology of secularization

The literal meaning of 'secularization' is the putting of church property to worldly use, and in a transferred sense the putting of religious terms to worldly use; according to the theory of the time this is society without the church, morality without religion, science without theology and man without God. Since the beginning of the Enlightenment, rationalism and revolution, both church and theology have condemned this fundamental development of the modern European world as apostasy from God, as rebellion against religion, and atheism which must lead to anarchy. Only after the Second World War did a critical theology come into being which had a positive attitude to secularization and only rejected secularism.

Dietrich Bonhoeffer had the most powerful effect with his ideas about the 'world come of age'. For him secularization had the positive significance of the de-divinization of the world and the discovery of its wordliness. God as a moral, political, scientific working hypothesis to explain the world was obsolete. We cannot be honest without recognizing that we have to live in the world even if there is no God (*etsi Deus non daretur*). So theology is wrong if it wants to attempt to introduce 'God' as an explanation of areas in nature which have not yet been worked out or as a refuge from moral or political problems which have not been overcome. Theology must take account of the worldliness of the world and welcome as progress the fact that human beings are free and have come of age. This, however, is possible only if the theology of the modern world offers its own interpretation more definitely than before. For Bonhoeffer the religious interpretation of the world was already superseded by Christian faith in the incarnation of God: God has entered into the reality of the world and no longer stands over against it. Life in the world 'without God' was disclosed radically by the way in which God abandoned the Son of God

16

on the cross. The God of the Bible gains power in the world by his powerlessness. 'Only the suffering God can help.' So in the light of the Christian knowledge of the incarnate and crucified God Bonhoeffer judged that 'the world come of age is more godless and therefore perhaps nearer to God than the world which has not come of age'. The modern religionless world certainly brings the religious age of Christianity to an end, but at the same time it opens up the possibilites of authentic Christian faith. The Enlightenment made mediaeval 'natural theology' impossible and forced Christian theology back on itself.

Friedrich Gogarten also developed a theology of the secularized world, but he began from anthropology. As a result of modern science the world of nature is de-divinized, de-demonized and made the world of human beings. In this way the sciences fulfil the command given at creation: 'Subdue the earth.' Science liberates human beings from the powers and laws of nature and makes them its lord. But if human subjects can no longer understand themselves in terms of the powerful secular ordinances, how can they understand themselves? Gogarten's answer is that through faith, human beings ground their existence in the transcendent God and understand themselves in terms of him, not of the world. In Christian terms they become 'sons of God'. But if in communion with Christ they are raised to this divine sonship, then they also become heirs of the world which God entrusts to them. The anthropology of Christian faith and the new possibilities offered by science and technology converge in the position of human beings 'between God and the world'. Science and technology hominize the world; Christian faith in the son humanizes men and women: anyone who lives wholly from God is free in the face of the whole world. Conversely, this freedom from the world and this power over the world is proved only through faith. True faith in God is the basis for the secular autonomy

17

of human beings and prevents modern men and women from taking refuge in ideologies and dictatorships for fear of their freedom.

The American theologian Harvey Cox attempted a theology for the 'secular city'. The collapse of traditional religion and morality and the rise of a new urban civilization coincide and characterize the modern world. In sociological terms secularization simply means urbanization. In the modern conurbation (megalopolis, technopolis) nature is de-divinized, history is de-fatalized, religion is privatized, morality becomes pluralistic and men and women become increasingly mobile. The modern conurbation becomes a melting pot of races, peoples, religions and cultures. It is the social reality of the religionless, rationalistic and pluralistic age. So far the traditional churches have not found an answer to the challenges of the modern conurbation. They usually transfer the relationships of the tribe and the village to the city. If Christianity wants to find a place in the city, then fundamental transformations are needed: the church must understand itself dynamically as a voluntary avant-garde of the kingdom of God; theology must become theology of social change; Christian faith must develop powers of cultural exorcism. In the anonymity of the conurbation only personal faith provides assurance of one's identity. By prophetic proclamation the gospel frees people from the new gods and demons of the consumer society and politics. Through Christian communities the church heals the socially wounded and sick. The new 'political theology' took up these beginnings. It agreed with the secular world on two basic ideas:

1. The recognition of the radical wordliness of the world is simply an insight into its historicity. If modern men and women no longer experience reality in the rhythm of nature, but as open history, then only hope for the future provides meaning for enduring and creating this history. In Christianity the future of history has always been expressed by the symbol of the

kingdom of God. Within this eschatological horizon, church and world no longer stand over against each other but are caught up on a common course. The modern orientation on the future is based on the biblical faith in the promise. This becomes secular in it. The modern world calls forth faith as hope and theology as the basis of the future (eschatology).

2. The modern primacy of praxis over knowledge is bound up with the recognition of the historicity of the world. Moral and political praxis verifies theories, just as it also leads to new theories. Modern criticism of religion no longer investigates the nature of religion, but only its practical, psychological and political functions. So theology under the conditions of the modern world can no longer be pure theory, but must become practical theory. It is necessarily 'political theology', reflection on praxis in the light of the gospel – faith becoming practical in the cause of public justice. Both the eschatological orientation of theology and its political situation lead not only into the secular age but also beyond the bounds of the bourgeois religion of this age.

3. The 'Third World' and the theology of liberation

With the exception of China, the liberation of peoples from European colonialism after the Second World War did not bring them liberation from the economic imperialism of the industrial countries. In the period from 1956 to 1966 it was believed that the under-development of the peoples of the 'Third World' could be overcome by politics of development and development aid. Although the idea of development is still dominant in politics and the church, as early as 1968, at the Conference of Latin American Bishops in Medellin, it was shown to be an illusion. The gap between the 'First World' and the 'Third World' is growing, and underdevelopment is proving to be development in reverse: the dependence and

19

indebtedness of Third World peoples is getting out of control. In order to convey the real situation more accurately the ideology of development was replaced by dependence theory. This is the reversal of Lenin's theory of imperialism and demonstrates that the overall development of the world always benefits the centres and conurbations of power, while the poor are increasingly marginalized. As a result of the division of work in the world economy, mono-cultures are being forcibly created in those countries for the world market, and as a result of this the indigenous subsistence-economies are being destroyed. The modern conurbations are impoverishing the land and making it a cultural wilderness. Today's 'Third World' is producing the proletariat of world society.

For a while the churches looked for a 'theology of development' and an ethics to match. Then, above all in Latin America, first a 'theology of revolution' came into being and then the 'theology of liberation', which takes its analysis of the situation from dependence theory, came into being in order to introduce the churches and the peoples to the struggle for liberation from this oppression. Its basic ideas derive partly from the European theology of hope and political theology, but its starting point and determining factors are different, because they lie in the situation of the poor and oppressed of the 'Third World'. Here theology takes the radical form of critical reflection on praxis in the light of the gospel. 'Praxis' is primarily the experience of life as it is lived, in this case the people's experience of poverty, exploitation and brutal oppression. So critical theology seeks first of all to disclose the setting of the church in the life of the people: is it a power of repression and an accomplice of domination, or is it the home of the poor and a power for their liberation? Power struggles and class struggles in Latin America show to what degree this question splits the churches themselves into a church of the rulers and a church of the people. If theology reflects on the existence of the church in the light of

20

Jesus' gospel of the kingdom of God for the poor, then it must become a theology which is critical of society and critical of the church. It cannot just interpret the world in a different way; it has to want to change it. So it leads with an intrinsic necessity to a new praxis: the liberation of the oppressed. The 'theology of liberation' is not only another theology over against traditional theology but another way of doing theology. It is an eminently practical theory: first comes orthopraxis, then orthodoxy; first comes historical commitment to the liberation of the oppressed, then comes theological reflection. Therefore theological theory understands itself as an element in the struggle for liberation which changes the world. Its goal is the creation of a just society in solidarity which is to be a historical parable of the coming divine kingdom of justice and peace.

Since 1968 the 'theology of liberation' which developed above all in Latin America has spread increasingly widely. Its method of action and reflection was adopted both by 'Black Theology' in the USA (James Cone) and in South Africa (Allan Boesak) and by 'feminist theology' (Rosemary Ruether). Wherever classes, races, sexes or individual groups in this society become aware of their subjection, humiliation and exploitation, the method of liberation theology offers itself as a way to a better future. In many parts of the world the exploitation of the poor, the humiliation of the coloured, the oppression of women and the displacement of the handicapped form a vicious circle which brings misery and death to millions.

Special attention should be paid to the feminist theology of liberation, because the oppression of women continues in cultures which came into being as a result of the displacement of the early matriarchy by aggressive patriarchy. This includes all so-called high cultures and world religions that we know. The Old Testament is a telling example of the replacement of Canaanite fertility cults by the Yahwistic religion of the fathers. Even the Christianity of the early church is religious testimony

21

to male predominance, although both men and women were baptized equally. The feminist theology of liberation which is coming into being today is the herald of a far-reaching cultural revolution the consequences of which we cannot as yet see. The question is whether and to what degree such a theology of women's liberation can take up biblical and Christian traditions or, if that is not possible, whether it will break away from Christianity. Jesus' own liberation of women and his respect from them is the strongest motivation for a Christian emancipation of women. Feminist theology is concerned not only with the liberation of women from male superiority sanctioned by religion but also with the liberation of the body from the superiority of the soul and the liberation of nature from exploitation by humankind. Where feminist theology is successful, with women's liberation it therefore also leads to a new acceptance of human corporeality and a new communion with the natural environment. Like the Latin American theology of liberation, it too has an intrinsic tendency towards universal liberation. Basically all liberation theologies, no matter what their particular starting points, are concerned with the 'human emancipation of human beings': otherwise they would not be theologies.

Nevertheless questions remain: does not this new functionalization of theology into 'liberation theologies' lead to a neglect of the content of theology? Certainly we find a new way of doing theology, but so far there are very few new theological insights. Does the primacy of praxis over theory call for a new Christian dispositional ethics which ideologizes Christian faith? However, despite these critical questions it must be maintained that Christian faith is essentially messianic faith, and messianic faith is always liberating faith. For all its ideological borrowing, the 'theology of liberation' is still Christian theology.

4. Christian theology of modernity

Generally speaking, the theologies of the Middle Ages were all theologies of love. The theologies of the Reformers Luther, Zwingli and Calvin were decidedly theologies of faith. But the basic question of modern times is the question of the future. Therefore Christian theology of modernity must necessarily be a theology of the future. According to Kant, pure reason gives the answer to the question 'What can I know?' Practical reason gives the answer to the question 'What shall I do?' Religion should give the answer to the third question, 'What may I hope for?' But if it is to answer this question about hope, Christian theology must be developed in terms of eschatology (the doctrine of the last things). The traditional doctrine of the rescue of the soul into a heaven beyond must become the doctrine of the future of the kingdom of God which renews heaven and earth. The traditional other-worldly hope must be supplemented by hope for the transformation and renewal of the earth. The attitude of passive waiting must become creative hope, which now already anticipates what will be tomorrow. The physical and material components of the Christian resurrection hope are being rediscovered. The cosmic dimensions of hope for the new creation are also being developed. Only then will criticism of the present and its transformation be possible.

In the nineteenth century human hope was largely concerned with belief in progress. Progress was taken for granted by most movements in science and culture. After the catastrophes of the twentieth century this secular faith has been deeply shaken and often turned into its opposite; the feeling that the world is coming to an end is spreading. Today it is the task of theology to formulate liberating hope in such a way that it is neither caught up into immanent belief in progress nor decays into apocalyptic anxiety about the future. The

Christian hope of the kingdom of God supports and mobilizes all inner-worldly hopes for more freedom and better justice, but it also criticizes the human hybris in them. Therefore it also resists the modern distortion of hope into resignation. Beyond hybris and resignation, hope in God guarantees the stamina of patience in history and the power for rebirth from that defeat. The new orientation of theology on the future has proved itself in Christian-Marxist dialogues and in the dialogue with modern theories of history and modern scientific theories.

Theology in modern times will necessarily be a theology of freedom. The modern world came into being as a result of freedom movements and is further caught up in such movements. Because church and theology clung too long to the traditional 'authoritarian principle', many freedom movements sided with atheism. If Christian theology wants to get the better of modern atheism, it must first overcome the impact of atheism and show that the biblical God of the exodus of the people and the resurrection of Christ does not get in the way of human freedom, but is rather the basis for it, preserves and defends it. A Christianity which is based on these biblical traditions of freedom would indeed become what Hegel called a 'religion of freedom'. But it will have to overcome the old theocratic theism and the authoritarian principle in the churches which is legitimated by it. Only then would the Christian 'religion of freedom' also be in a position to fight convincingly against the perversions of freedom in the modern world – anarchy and despotism – and overcome them. However, as long as belief in God and the authority of the church treat men and women as immature and irresponsible children, any theological criticism of the modern history of freedom will lack credibility.

The freedoms which must be recognized by and grounded in theology include:

1. Freedom of religion. It was a great step forward when in the Second Vatican Council the Catholic Church explicitly

recognized the freedom of religion which it had earlier rejected.

2. Freedom of belief. Modern men and women believe on the basis of their own hearing of the gospel and their own decision, not because they are forced to belong to a church, however much they owe the communication of the gospel to the church and take their place in the wider communion of believers. In personal faith they seek and find their inner identity, which frees them from social and political pressures.

3. Freedom of conscience. Men and women come of age are responsible for their own lives. Therefore they must act in accordance with their consciences. The churches can sharpen human consciences, but they cannot relieve anyone of his or her conscience and decide in their stead.

4. Freedom of association. In modern society the churches can no longer organize themselves as great institutions; they must organize themselves in communities of the people. Churches are alive only to the degree that communities are alive. The future of the church lies in the community in which all members perceive the universal priesthood of believers, with their capabilities and possibilities. The specific ministry of the priest or pastor is embedded in the community of believers. Clerical theism and laicistic atheism cease in the voluntary communities which are coming into being today in the basic communities.

5. Freedom of theology. Theology is the common task of all Christianity, not just the specific task of trained specialists. Christian theology always has a responsibility to the church. But it may not be subjected to the powers prevailing in the church at any time. Christian theology also has a responsibility to human beings in the world. However, it may not hand itself over to particular social ideologies. The freedom of theology as responsible to the church and the world is the presupposition

that it takes up the problems of this age independently and contributes towards their solution from its own power.

4. In search of Christian identity

As long as the church was at home in the *Corpus Christianum*, its Christian identity was not in question, but taken for granted. It enjoyed universal recognition on religious and moral, social and political levels. In the unitary culture of the mediaeval Catholic world and the unitary culture of the bourgeois Protestant world the church was an integral element of a historical form of Christianity. By 'Christianity' here I mean cultural syntheses of church and state, faith and religion, theology and philosophy. They mould life in particular periods and particular regions; when their forms become obsolete, because they are no longer up to the challenges of the future, they collapse. The Christian identity of these cultural syntheses then becomes questionable. Questions have again to be asked about the origin and truth of Christian faith. Clandestinely since the beginning of modern times, but publicly since the French Revolution, Christianity in Europe, whether Catholic or Protestant, has found itself in an identity crisis which heralds the end of the *Corpus Christianum*. For a long time this crisis was sensed only vaguely and usually repressed. But the repressions of this identity crisis were themselves a sign of it and not a solution. They led to the fossilization of the forms of Christian life and to the death of its content. Here I mention only a few typical reactions.

The church has often responded to the displacement of the church from public life in modern times by making church life more ecclesiastical and by clericalizing the church, taking Christian existence into a social ghetto. The church has complained about the godlessness of the modern world and limited itself to the faithful remnant, the little flock. In the view

26

of many of our contemporaries, instead of being the dominant religion of the Christian West the church has become a sect on the periphery of modern society. Symptoms of a sectarian mentality in the churches today are a preservation of tradition without the founding of new traditions, a rigorous biblicism without the gospel preaching of liberation and an intolerant and anxious attitude in controversies within the churches. In that case one can only formulate Christian identity in contrast to the 'world'. A friend-foe mentality is developing between the 'church' and the 'world'. Christian identity is no longer open and inviting but anxious and aggressive. In certain Christian groups this aggressive Christian identity is accentuated, giving rise to the apocalyptic division between the righteous and the godless in which the end of the world, the apocalyptic Armageddon, is announced. Theologians have often reacted in a similar way to the displacement of traditional theology from academic discussion and public cultural discourse: they have neglected to make the necessary innovations. That is why the modern history of theology is dominated by so many repristinations of the past: neo-Thomism, neo-Calvinism, neo-Orthodoxy, the Augustine renaissance, the Luther renaissance, the Aquinas renaissance, and many more. Certainly these traditions contain still unsuspected treasures, but are they up to the challenges of our time?

The quest for what is originally and indivisibly Christian is of another kind. It is the way *ad fontes*. This way is bound up with a concern to reform the church and theology and to renew Christian existence in the truth of its origin, in order to arrive at authentic testimony in the present.

In Catholic theology this development began under the pontificate of Leo XIII. About the turn of the century Catholic scholarship came into being. There was a return from the fossilized formulae of faith in the present to the living theological traditions of the Middle Ages and the patristic period;

these were studied without prejudice by means of the methods of modern historical research. These Christian traditions led back to the Bible itself. The first scientific, historical-critical exegesis in the Catholic Church came into being (A.Loisy, M.-L.Lagrange, L.Duchesne, and so on). Granted, the application of modern historical-critical methods also brought results which tended to put church tradition and the contemporary doctrine of the church in question. The 'modernist crisis' developed, and in 1907 Pius X took magisterial action against it with the 'anti-modernist oath', though he did not resolve it. Nevertheless there was an upsurge of critical historical scholarship. With it a reformed Catholic biblical movement came into being. The spirit of the renewal of the church and theology from the truth of its origin then continued in the Second Vatican Council. In this way the defensive mentality which followed the modernist crisis was overcome in the Catholic Church. Biblical scholarship found that place which was its due because of the truth of the origin of Christian theology. Through it Catholic theology entered the ecumenical community with Protestant and Orthodox theology, for the nearer a theology gets to the truth of its origins, the more ecumenical it becomes. Catholic biblical scholarship has found its place in ecumenical biblical scholarship. Even though the study of scripture does not have the same basic significance for dogmatic theology in the Catholic Church as it does in the Protestant Church, nevertheless as the Council affirmed, it should be the soul of all theology.

In Protestant theology things were different, because biblical scholarship as historical-critical research into the foundation documents of the Christian faith had already begun around a century earlier. The central problem here was not the relationship between the Bible and church tradition, but the relationship between Christ and the Bible. The historical-critical investigation of the Bible had been guided since Reimarus and Semler

(1778, 1779) by an interest in getting to know Jesus himself and understanding him as he really was. The historical investigation of the life of Jesus led to the liberation of the historical figure of Jesus from the dogma of Christ and to the liberation of faith from dogma. The christological dogma of Chalcedon had to be overturned so that people could seek the historical Jesus, and only through the search for the real historical Jesus could the christological dogma be overturned. People looked for the historical Jesus in order to encounter his real personality and to come to know what was originally and indivisibly Christian. For Jesus himself is the origin and the identity of the Christian. Albert Schweitzer gave a classic account of the 'quest of the historical Jesus' (1906): 'It is a uniquely great act of truthfulness, one of the most significant events in the whole spiritual life of humankind.' However, the result of the quest was ambiguous. People had gone out to find the historical Jesus and thought that they could then bring him into our own time as he really is, as teacher and saviour. Historical-critical research broke the bonds with which for centuries he had been fettered to the rocks of church doctrine and rejoiced when they saw the historical person of Jesus coming to them: 'However, he did not stay, but passed by our time and returned to his own.' Historical-critical research in fact discovered that Jesus is a stranger to our time and our cultural wishes, as it recognized the eschatological message of the kingdom of God, soon to break into the human world as the centre of his whole historical existence. If Jesus understood himself completely in terms of this message from God, then the origin of the church's christology already lies in Jesus himself: true man and true God.

Lastly, historical research into the life of Jesus did not lead to a humanistic alternative to the church's proclamation of Christ, but took this back to its origin and inner criterion of truth: the proclaimed Christ is Jesus of Nazareth. What is to be regarded as 'Christian' must therefore be demonstrated from Jesus himself and his message. Jesus himself, and no one else, is not only the origin but also the principle of all Christian theology. He is the criterion for discerning the spirits. He is the canon in the canon, the inner principle of distinction in the New Testament. The more Protestant biblical scholarship followed this principle and understood the Reformation slogan *sola scriptura* as the outward representation of the truly Christian principle of the *solus Christus*, the more it had an effect on Catholic biblical scholarship and the beginnings of Orthodox biblical scholarship and itself became ecumenical. The way *ad fontes* led on the Catholic side to the discovery of the Bible as the origin and criterion of the church's tradition. On the Protestant side it led to the discovery of Jesus as the origin and criterion of the New Testament traditions. Those reforms of theology and church which in our century make known the authentic Christian identity begin from both these discoveries. The rediscovery of the Bible has brought the Old Testament into the foreground with a vengeance. So I shall first describe the significance of the new Christian 'theology of the Old Testament' for theology and the church. Historical research into the New Testament has reopened the christological question. So secondly I shall describe this discussion.

1. The significance of the Old Testament

Historically speaking, Christianity emerged out of Judaism. The New Testament presupposes the Old. Therefore the theological definition of the relationship between the New Testament and the Old and the significance of the Old Testament for the church is concerned with nothing less than Christian identity in relationship to Judaism. Why does the Christian church keep the Hebrew Bible of Israel as its 'Old Testament', and with what eyes do Christians read the Old Testament?

30

In 1923 the liberal Protestant theologian Adolf von Harnack asserted: 'To reject the Old Testament in the second century was a mistake which the mainstream church rightly repudiated; to retain it in the sixteenth century was a fate which the Reformation could not yet avoid; but to continue to keep it in Protestantism as a canonical document after the nineteenth century is the consequence of religious and ecclesiastical paralysis.' Here Harnack was only demonstrating the confusion of the Christian church and theology over the Old Testament. Does the Old Testament belong to the canon as a matter of theological necessity or only by the chances of history? Has it a message of its own for the church of Christ? What does it mean for the relationship of the church to the synagogue and to Israel? Christian theology has developed a series of divergent standpoints in connection with the Old Testament.

(a) The standpoint of religious indifference

From the perspective of Christianity, Judaism and paganism are alien religions. The church addresses all men and women as a 'religion of redemption', no matter whether they are Jews or pagans, for they are all equal in their need for redemption. There would be a Christian religion of redemption even if there had never been an Israel, and there would continue to be one if there were no more Jews. The Old Testament is bound up with the New Testament only as a matter of historical chance. Since Christ the redeemer has appeared, it no longer has anything special to say. This is the standpoint represented by the influential Protestant theologian Friedrich Schleiermacher in his influential book *The Christian Faith*: 'Christianity is indeed in a special historical relationship with Judaism, but as far as its historical existence and its purpose is concerned, its relations with Judaism and paganism are equal' (§12). But if the Old Testament is only the book of faith of a Jewish religion, then it is hard to see why the Christian church retains it and does not

31

exchange it, say, for the religious writings of other people among whom it lives. Only when the so-called 'German Christians' under Hitler sought to replace the Old Testament with the Germanic sagas of the Edda did many theologians become clear about the irreplaceable significance of the Old Testament for Christian faith and Christian theology.

(b) The standpoint of the contrast necessary for salvation

From this perspective Christianity came into being as the result of a fundamental conflict with Judaism and continues to be involved in this conflict. The Old Testament reveals the law of God and the New Testament the gospel of God; the Old Testament teaches the law of retribution and the New Testament teaches the spirit of love; the Old Testament is valid only for the elect people of the Jews, the New Testament is open to all. Old and New Testaments, Israel and the church are seen as being in conflict, but this conflict is said to be necessary so that the newness of the New Testament and the special character of the church can be recognized. This standpoint is often adopted by theologians of the Lutheran tradition. As the latest of them, the New Testament scholar Rudolf Bultmann called the history of Israel attested in the Old Testament a 'history of failure', of the failure of this people before God, his law and his election, so as to put positive emphasis on justifying faith in Christ. 'To be certain of itself faith needs to know the significance of the law; otherwise it would succumb to being led astray by the law... The situation of the one who is justified emerges only on the basis of failure.' But that means that Christian faith needs to recall the law of God only as a negative background and preserves the stories of the Old Testament as a deterrent, to safeguard itself. From this standpoint Christian theology develops a theology of the Old Testament as a negative theology, in order to put itself in the right light. Unfortunately this contrasting of Christianity with Judaism has been widely disseminated by popular preaching: on the one hand the good Samaritan, on the other the self-righteous Pharisee; on the one hand the church with sight, on the other the blind synagogue.

(c) The standpoint of the legacy of salvation history

From this standpoint the history of Israel is only the 'prehistory' of Christianity and the Old Testament is a 'prelude' to the New. The people of Israel provided the preparation in salvation history for the coming of the church of the nations. Since the coming of Christ the church has taken the place of Israel, for in the New Testament we find the fulfilment of the Old. As the Lutheran theologian Paul Althaus put it: 'The church is certainly grounded in Israel as the elect people of God, but Israel also issues in the church. The church is now the true people of God.' We find the same thing in the Second Vatican Council's Declaration on the Relation of the Church to Non-Christian Religions: 'The Church of Christ acknowledges that in God's plan of salvation the beginning of her faith and election is to be found in the patriarchs, Moses and the prophets. She professes that the salvation of the Church is mysteriously prefigured in the exodus of God's chosen people from the land of bondage... She believes that Christ has through his cross reconciled Jews and Gentiles and made them one in himself.' This view is the one that is most widespread. It represents Christianity as the consummation of Judaism and as the faith that supersedes it. Here Judaism has no place of its own alongside the church in God's salvation history. As the Old Testament of the church the Torah has lost its significance for Israel.

(d) The standpoint of the prophetic community

From this standpoint there is a recognition of the special and distinctive features of the Old Testament in that 'surplus' of promises of the future which are not yet universally fulfilled in the coming of Christ and the experience of the Spirit, but are only implemented in principle. These are the promises of the kingdom of God which renews heaven and earth, the kingdom of freedom which brings peace to all creation. The New Testament proclaims not only the fulfilment or the abolition of these real future promises of the Old Testament but their confirmation by Christ and their dissemination by the church to all peoples. Joachim di Fiore already put forward this view in the twelfth century. It is alive in the tradition of Reformed theology. In the surplus of its promises the Old Testament has an added value over against the New. Through the message of the New Testament, people from all nations are taken into the hopes of Israel. The future of the New Testament is the same as the future of the Old: both Testaments focus on the kingdom of God. Only in this view is the Old Testament taken with theological seriousness. The special significance of the synagogue and Israel alongside the church of Christ is also recognized. Jews and Christians together have 'one book and one hope' (Martin Buber).

Christianity does not gain its original identity through the negation, repudiation or inheriting of Judaism, but only in the community of the promises of God and the hopes of Israel. The more recent Old Testament theology of G. von Rad, W. Zimmerli and others is the bridge to the common origin of Christians and Jews and the pointer towards their common future. The church of the nations also reads the Torah of Israel as the book of its hope for the kingdom of God. It finds in the messiah Jesus, in accordance with the testimony of the New Testament, access to this hope.

34

2. *The christological question and the New Testament*

The name of Jesus Christ denotes what is special about Christianity. This name certainly sounds like a double name, but in fact it is one name and one title: Christ is God's messiah. So the critical theological question runs: Is Jesus really the Christ? Has God's messiah appeared in Jesus of Nazareth?

Since the earliest confessions of faith the church has taken the New Testament as proof of its dogma of Christ: Jesus Christ is God's only Son. The New Testament became the basis for the church's teaching of Christ, christology. From antiquity, however, this christology has been christology from above: it begins in heaven, and then with the incarnation of the Son of God descends to the history of Jesus of Nazareth, goes with him, the incarnate Son of God, from Galilee to Jerusalem, sees him dying on the cross on Golgotha, experiences his resurrection from the dead on the third day, sees him ascend to heaven and expects his return for the last judgment at the end of days. This christological scheme of the descent of the redeemer to earth and his ascent to heaven is an old, religious, pre-Christian myth. It was applied at an early stage (Phil.2) to the career of Jesus, from God to humankind and from humankind to God. But does this christological myth correspond to Jesus himself?

Until modern times people felt and thought in metaphysical terms: they were certain beyond question of the existence of the incorruptible God; only transitory beings were regarded as uncertain and questionable. So their christological question was not whether Jesus is God but whether he is really and truly man.

However, the 'anthropological shift' in modern thought has reversed the christological question: it is not the humanity of Jesus that is questionable but his divinity. The existence of God in heaven can no longer be presupposed in order to recognize

Jesus of Nazareth as the incarnate Son of God. It is necessary to start from the other end, from the man Jesus of Nazareth, in order to come to know God. Therefore christology under the conditions of modern thought is constantly and programmatically christology from below. The view of the career of Jesus 'from above' can only be God's standpoint. Human beings live below on earth and know only within the sphere of their own possibilities of experience. They are encountered, not by the eternal Son of God in heaven, but by the man Jesus of Nazareth. From his message of God and his relationship to God it may then become evident to them who God the Father is. The old christology 'from above' was always christology of the 'God-man' Christ: divine and human nature in one person. By contrast, the modern shift towards christology from below begins with Jesus, the 'man of God'. His divinity consists in the constant power of his awareness of God. His sinless humanity is the demonstration of his divinity. His redemptive work consists in strengthening our troubled awareness of God (Friedrich Schleiermacher), so we must let his humanity in his historical personality work on us in order to recognize the being of God in his unique consciousness of God (Wilhelm Herrmann).

'Christology from below' is always a christology of humanity. Some trends in this modern christology saw the humanity of Jesus in his exemplary religious consciousness. In this they followed Schleiermacher. Others stressed his exemplary morality, following Kant and Ritschl. Today people are fond of stressing Jesus' exemplary humanity: Jesus is the authentic norm in that he is wholly devoted to God and to his fellow human beings. As his disciples, men and women can truly live human lives in the world of today.

But does not this modern anthropological christology presuppose the old theological christology? How could a christology 'from below' begin if it did not presuppose an 'above' which it hopes to reach? Why should Jesus of Nazareth in particular play an exemplary and normative role for true humanity alongside Buddha, Socrates and other great figures in world history had he not been proclaimed with divine authority? The modern 'christology from below' is a significant correction to that old 'christology from above', but it cannot exist on its own without collapsing. Any 'christology' already presupposes God by using the title Christ, and indeed presupposes the God of Israel, the God of hope. Therefore today in modern theology we have the great fronts between the theological 'christology from above' as developed recently by Karl Barth and Karl Rahner and the anthropological 'christology from below', as it has recently been put forward by Hans Küng. Despite magisterial decisions on this question, however, this is not an alternative. Here are perspectives which mutually supplement each other. Both christologies are to be related dialectically; otherwise we have a christology without Jesus and a Jesuology without Christ.

If we go back to the New Testament traditions we find that the history of Jesus Christ is always illuminated from two sides: it is narrated in the light of his historical mission, and it is recalled in the light of his eschatological resurrection. These are not the metaphysical perspectives 'from above' and 'from below' but the historical perspectives of forward-looking hope and backward-looking recollection. The (Synoptic) Gospels tell the story of Jesus in the light of his messianic mission and his message of the kingdom of God. They depict his life as the consequence of his message. His mission is fulfilled in his suffering and death on the cross on Golgotha. By contrast the apostolic letters begin from the resurrection of Christ and proclaim the Lord present in the Spirit. Only occasionally, in the eucharistic tradition, does Paul return to the earthly Jesus. Of course the Gospels also relate the history of the sending of Jesus in the light of his resurrection, otherwise his history would never have been told. Of course Paul also recalls the history of the risen Lord in the light of his messianic mission. Both perspectives, forwards and backwards, expand and correct each other: nothing can be proclaimed of the risen Lord which contradicts the earthly Jesus; the earthly crucified Jesus remains the sole criterion for any proclamation of Christ, for Jesus is Lord and no one else. Nor can anything be told of the earthly Jesus which goes against the proclamation of the Risen Christ and the experience of his presence in the Spirit: the risen Lord remains the presupposition for any recollection and narrative of the history of Jesus.

The point at which the history of Jesus and the proclamation of Christ coincide is the cross on Golgotha. In the light of Jesus' life his death is the end of his messianic mission. In the light of his resurrection, however, his death is his true beginning and the beginning of the kingdom of God on earth. Therefore in contrast to the old christology 'from above' and the modern christology 'from below', recent theology has brought the cross of Jesus Christ more markedly into the centre of christology and Christian theology generally. The cross of Christ makes manifest who the true God is; the cross of Christ makes manifest who real humanity is. In the crucified Jesus the God of humanity and the humanity of God are equally recognized. Christian theology is at heart a theology of the cross. That means that any theology must be tested by its reply to the cry of the dying Jesus: 'My God, my God, why hast thou forsaken me?' The most recent developments in theology have begun their thinking by putting this question of Jesus to God alongside the question of Christ. In this way they have also taken up the question about God which suffering humankind poses in the present day.

That which was originally, truly and distinctively Christian has always been marked in all Christian churches with the sign of the cross. The crucified Christ who redeems by his death and calls people to discipleship through his spirit is the only norm in Christianity. In him God identifies himself with innocent and suffering humankind. In him men and women find their liberating, true identity which is in the image of God.

In the present disintegration of the customs of the Christian world and what it takes for granted, Christian identity becomes uncertain and questionable. Christians and churches are thrown back on what is original and essential in their faith. On the way to the truth of their origins they rediscover the Bible: dogmatic theology has to be grounded in biblical theology if it is to give an answer to the question of the origin and nature of Christianity. This necessity frees theology from the cultural environment of milieu-Catholicism and the Protestant bourgeois world, puts it on its own feet and makes it distinctly Christian and definitely kerygmatic in its statements. In the original and essential biblical testimony to Christian faith, theology finds the one who makes it Christian theology: Jesus, the Christ of God. His messianic mission, his surrender to death on the cross and his resurrection to new eternal life are the sources for any relevant Christian existence today: Jesus Christ is not an object of theology but the one and all-determining subject of any theology which claims to be Christian.

5. Theology in an 'ecumenical age'

With the collapse of the Roman empire Christianity, which had a unitary organization within it, collapsed too. In 1054 the Eastern and Western churches, Byzantium and Rome, split, and East and West went different ways. In the schism which followed the Reformation in the sixteenth century the unity of the Christian West also disintegrated. Politically that was the beginning of the wars of religion; theologically it was the rise of the 'confessional era'. Europe achieved its political peace after the Thirty Years' War only through the development of the modern, confessionally neutral, secular state and the spread of a culture of religious tolerance. The 'secular age' dissolved the traditional forms of the *Corpus Christianum* by the necessary division of church and state. As a result of this, all the Christian churches of Europe were compelled to stand on their own feet and co-operate increasingly with one another. The first historical response of Christianity to the end of the old *Corpus Christianum* and the beginning of the secular age was the missionary movement of the eighteenth and nineteenth centuries, the greatest missionary movement in the history of Christianity; the second was the ecumenical movement, which after the centuries-long history of splits and divisions marked the beginning of a new age of collaboration, community and union between of the various Christian churches. The missionary movement and the ecumenical movement came into being together and belong together. They both freed the churches from European provincialism and confessional particularism and put them on the way to being a universal church of the nations.

The entry of the churches into the 'ecumenical age' had considerable consequences for church theologies, but these were slow in making themselves felt. The church theologies could now no longer serve only the self-understanding of their own confessions and mark them off from other confessions. Previous Catholic and Protestant theologies had to understand themselves as stages on the way towards a common Christian theology. In the earlier 'confessional age' theology served to safeguard the identity of a particular confession. It was therefore always 'controversial theology', and in the so-called 'distinctive doctrines' of confessions brought out what separated one confession from another. In the 'ecumenical age' these different church theologies have to seek common ground in order to make possible the co-existence and collaboration of the churches which is needed. This does not lead to confessional syncretism or to theological indifference to the truth, but to reflection on essentials. The question of the true church comes into the foreground. Any one confession in search of the true church in its own form of the church will also have to look for it in all other forms of the church. Despite divisions and mutual condemnations, the awareness of the oneness of the church has remained alive in all Christian churches, as long as Christ has been confessed as the One Lord of the Church. Therefore the change in theology from confessional stubbornness to ecumenical harmony has been easier than many people had expected. Theology today has become so much the common task of all Christian churches that it is often no longer possible to recognize the confessional origin of the different contributions.

As an example of the course of theology in the 'ecumenical age' I have taken the development of the ecumenical department 'Faith and Order' in the World Council of Churches in Geneva, which was founded in 1927. The movements for world mission and the Movement for Practical Christianity had already come into being previously. There was a simple slogan for the collaboration of the churches in mission and diaconia: 'Doctrine divides, service unites.' The praxis of love, not the theological doctrine of faith, seemed to be a favourable field for collaboration and community. So it was a risk in 1927 to seek this community in the sphere of theological teaching and church order also. At first the Roman Catholic Church declined to collaborate. After more than fifty years of work together it can be said that the attempt has been successful. For a long time Catholic theologians have participated as observers and advisers and now they are also involved as members. Orthodox theologians are represented in all groups. A first consensus on the important questions of baptism, eucharist and ministry is now being proposed.

This theological development began at the first ecumenical

conferences with an attempt at a 'comparative ecclesiology' (1937 Edinburgh Conference).

People got to know one another in the hope that a better understanding of differing views about faith and order would lead to a deepening of the desire for reunion and to official resolutions from the churches to this effect. The first surprising result was a kind of 'negative consensus': they discovered that the traditional distinctive doctrines of the church need not necessarily be seen as divisive. The distinctive doctrines of the various churches did not need to be formulated exclusively; they could also be formulated inclusively. They did not need to exclude others, but could also lead to the expansion and enrichment of others. The various theological traditions were preserved at this stage, but they took on a new status which was no longer confessional but ecumenical. There was no longer any reason for the separation of the churches, but it proved impossible to formulate common belief. The mutual condemnations of the sixteenth century were seen as being no longer relevant.

The 1952 Conference of the World Council of Churches at Lund was a turning point from comparative ecclesiology to a christological ecclesiology. 'We have recognized that we cannot make any real progress towards unity unless we compare our various conceptions of the nature of the church and the traditions in which they are incorporated. Rather, it has shown that we come closer to one another when we come closer to Christ. Therefore through our divisions we must move towards a deeper understanding of the unity of Christ given to us by God with his church.' Since then the ecumenical course has led from the various churches and theological traditions to an original tradition of Christian faith which is given the name of Christ. In this journey from the branching arms of the river to a common source the churches transcend their historical divisions and discover their fellowship with one another in the

42

one church of Christ. It is the christological concentration of theological discussions in particular which has led to the discovery of the ecumenical community in the one universal church. Their unity does not lie in the uniformity of their conceptions and religious customs, but in the eucharistic community of all Christians. The eucharist had always been the source of the church's power. Eucharistic communion is also the goal of any ecumenical communion of Christians. Therefore the documents on *Baptism, Eucharist and Ministry* presented to all the churches in 1981 are an appropriate way of formulating that positive theological convergence which will lead to full eucharistic communion.

The course of the ecumenical movement can be recognized fairly clearly: it led from anathema to dialogue. It continued on from dialogue to co-operation. It will lead from co-operation to the common confession of faith. Decisions about that can only be made by a universal Christian council. Certainly the idea of an ecumenical, pan-Christian council and the hope that all Christianity will speak in it with one voice are still in the realm of utopia. However, they cast their utopian light forward: the churches are now already beginning to live in a conciliar way, i.e. to enter into that communion with one another which leads to such a council.

'Conciliar life' is not life without conflicts, but a life which keeps taking up the conflicts which once led to separation and working towards their resolution. The resolution of conflicts by separating the parties in dispute can bring temporary peace, but it is not a solution to the real conflict. To resolve real conflicts it is necessary to resume communion. In conciliar life the problems within Catholicism or within Protestantism at the same time also become shared Christian problems. Each church participates in the inner problems of the others. The old principle of not meddling in one another's communions is thus abandoned.

43

The other ecumenical vision bound up with 'conciliar life' is the community of 'reconciled diversity'. This is practised above all by the great confessional world alliances, by the Lutheran World Federation, the World Alliance of Reformed Churches, the Methodist World Council and other associations. This expression stresses the right to independence in the church unity that is sought, but this unity is not watered down in reconciliation.

In the Second Vatican Council, and since then, the Roman Catholic Church has entered much more deeply into ecumenical communion with the Orthodox and Protestant churches than is evident from institutions and official declarations. Pope John XXIII opened up new possibilities for ecumenism by issuing an open invitation to the Second Vatican Council. The number of non-Roman Catholic 'observers' rose from forty in the first period of the council in 1962 to over a hundred in the fourth period in 1965. The Secretariat for Unity was founded as early as 1960. Because the 'observers' commented on the proceedings of the council in lectures and counsels of their own, they too played an active part in it, even in some council texts. In 1965 the French Roman Catholic conciliar theologian Yves Congar could rightly declare: 'The Catholic Church has finally entered the life of the ecumene, which begins where one is ready to stop thinking and living as though the others were not there and to join with them in the expectation of a day, even though it is still distant, when we can finally have full communion in the same bread of truth and the body of the Lord.' In the Council the Roman Catholic Church combined fidelity to itself with openness to the reality of the other Christian churches.

With their entry into the 'ecumenical age' the churches have set aside their absolutism, the conviction that they alone possess the truth of Christ, and their triumphalism, the attitude that they themselves are already 'heaven on earth'. Together they have put themselves on the road through history to that future which represents the fulfilment of history as the kingdom of God. That christological ecclesiology which goes from a variety of traditions to find one common origin has therefore led on the other side to that eschatological ecclesiology which understands the church as the historical people of God hoping for the consummation of the kingdom of God and moving towards it. It is this recognition of their own provisional nature in comparison to the kingdom of God which brings the various churches together on a common course.

This last notion has also drawn the attention of many theologians who think ecumenically to that first schism from which the Christian church itself emerged: to Israel and Judaism. The ecumenical movement is a great movement for conversion: the past separations and divisions of Christianity are done away with in order to gain the common future. In this way one finally arrives unavoidably at the first split between Christianity and Judaism. Without a new relationship to Judaism, synagogue and Israel the ecumenical movement will not achieve its goal. Without a new 'community of the way', made up of Christians and Jews, the people of God will not achieve any independent historical form. Dialogue with the Jews cannot therefore be carried on any longer within the framework of dialogue with 'non-Christian religions'; it has to be carried on in the centre of Christian theology. For too long, Christianity has only repudiated, rejected and persecuted Judaism in order to make itself into the true people of God in place of Israel. Entry into 'the ecumenical age' means not least a departure from all Christian antisemitism and the move to Christian Jewish communion. On the basis of the rediscovery of the significance of the Old Testament for the Christian church and on the basis of the Auschwitz holocaust, over the last twenty years in Europe there has been a wealth of Christian-Jewish conversations and a cautious, but theologically clear,

Christian recognition of Jewish faith. Christians and Jews are bound together much more closely in truth through the 'ecumene of the Bible' than they have so far been aware. Church and synagogue are the two sides of the living messianic hope for the one kingdom of God. The rediscovery of the significance of the Old Testament and the rediscovery of the Christian hope for the future have provided the theological basis for a new positive relationship between the churches and Judaism.

With its entry into its 'ecumenical age' the Christian church will also overcome its increasingly unrealistic cultural and political Eurocentrism and become universal. But if it becomes present in all peoples and cultures, it will inevitably find itself in conversation with the world religions. So far such conversations have taken place either to overwhelm the other religions in the service of Christian mission or out of purely academic interest in alien religious phenomena. Now, however, Christianity must be capable of dialogue and ready for dialogue if it is to survive and make its contribution to the future of humanity. Each religion once had its own history. Granted, the religions have different pasts, but today their future lies in their new fellowship. The theological concepts relating to the attitude of Christianity to the other world religions all still come from the pre-ecumenical age. There is still that church absolutism for which there is no salvation outside the church and therefore there can only be damnation in the other world religions. There is still the absolutism of faith for which non-Christian religions are nothing but idolatry and superstition. The syncretistic claim to totality with which Christianity has often enough taken over the possessions and ideas of other religions in order to absorb them into itself is not a real offer of dialogue. If Christianity wants to be capable of dialogue, it must overcome this absolutism and trust the truth of God more than its own representation of this truth. On the other hand, Christian faith cannot fall victim to a sceptical relativism which is not interested in a religious conversation with the world religions. A true community of world religions is conceivable only if the religions take part in a fruitful exchange and openly influence one another. Authentic interest in another religion arises if there is a creative need for the other. For Christians the dialogue with people of other religions is not a means to a predetermined end, but the basically neutral expression of its life in love and its wish for communion with others.

Finally, entry into the ecumenical age is also entry into the age of humanity. Today the nations have to be concerned for the development of a just world society and the realization of permanent world peace if they are to survive. Therefore it must be 'One world or no world'. The Christian church, which is now present in all peoples and cultures, can become a catalyst for the development of justice and peace on earth. Christians have therefore paid great attention to furthering the recognition and extension of human rights. All the major churches have involved themselves in human rights as a foundation for a future world society by making theological declarations. In the unity of individual and social, economic and ecological rights, human rights are the starting point for both an ethics and a politics of the coming world society. Here the churches will also become the expression of the world conscience over the most blatant violations of human rights in dictatorships and class societies. The more the churches today are aware of their old syntheses with particular peoples, states and classes and of their ecumenical fellowship and human responsibility, the more clearly they will become the prophetic factor in the politics of the world society to come. Their ecumenical universality gives them this new political responsibility.

It is only possible to talk meaningfully about a future for the nations when world peace has been established and secured.

Peace is the first condition for human survival. The more the church frees itself from the interests of the ruling nations and classes and gives its own testimony, the more it can do for the peace of all men and women. The ecumenical association of the separated churches is the basis for their contribution to world peace. Certainly all churches have spoken out for peace, but a theological doctrine of peace in an age of the threat of nuclear war and the growing ecological crisis is only in its infancy. In it the old doctrine of the 'just war' and 'human domination of nature' must be revised. Human rights and peace with nature are the most urgent political themes for theology at the end of the twentieth century.

Bibliography

Chapters 1 and 2: On the theology of the nineteenth and twentieth centuries

R.Aubert, *The Church in a Secularized Society*, London and New York 1978

G.Becher, *Theologie in der Gegenwart. Tendenzen und Perspektiven*, Regensburg 1978

K.Barth, *Protestant Theology in the Nineteenth Century*, London 1972

C.Geffré, *A New Age in Theology*, New York 1974

E.Hirsch, *Geschichte der neueren evangelischen Theologie, im Zusammenhang mit den allgemeinen Bewegungen des europäischen Denkens*, I-IV, Gütersloh 1949

F.W.Kantzenbach, *Programme der Theologie, Denker, Schulen, Wirkungen von Schleiermacher bis Moltmann*, Munich 1978

M.Neusch and B.Chenu, *Au pays de la théologie, à la découverte des hommes et des courants*, Paris 1979

M.Schoof, *A Survey of Catholic Theology, 1800-1970*, New York and London 1970

A.Kuyper, *Reformation wider Revolution*, Berlin 1904

C.Schmitt, *Politische Theologie. Vier Kapitel zur Lehre von der Demokratie*, Munich and Leipzig 1934

H.Arendt, *On Revolution*, London 1964

Chapter 3: On secular relevance

M.Horkheimer and T.W.Adorno, *Dialectic of Enlightenment*, London and New York 1973

P.Tillich, *Systematic Theology*, Vols 1-3, Chicago and Welwyn Garden City 1951ff., reissued London 1978

K.Rahner, *Theological Investigations* (20 vols.), London and New York 1961ff.

H.Blumenberg, *Die Legitimität der Neuzeit*, Frankfurt 1966

H.Küng, *On Being a Christian*, London and New York 1976

R.Bultmann, *Glauben und Verstehen* I-IV, Tübingen 1933-65 (there are English translations of I = *Faith and Understanding*, London and New York 1955; 2 = *Essays Philosophical and Theological*, London 1969)

H.W.Bartsch (ed.), *Kerygma und Mythos*, I-IV, Hamburg 1960ff. (selections have been translated into English, in *Kerygma and Myth*, London 1953; *Kerygma and Myth* 2, London 1962)

G.Ebeling, *Word and Faith*, London and Philadelphia 1963

P.Ricoeur, *The Conflict of Interpretation. Essays on Hermeneutics*, Evanston 1974

J.B.Metz, J.Moltmann and W.Oelmüller, *Kirche im Prozess der Aufklärung. Aspekte einer neuen politischen Theologie*, Munich 1970

D.Sölle, *Politische Theologie*, Stuttgart 1971

D.Bonhoeffer, *Letters and Papers from Prison. The Enlarged Edition*, London and New York 1971

F.Gogarten, *Der Mensch zwischen Gott und Welt*, Heidelberg 1952

T.Rendtorff, *Theorie des Christentums*, Gütersloh 1972

W.Pannenberg, *Theology and the Philosophy of Science*, London and Philadelphia 1974

N.Luhmann, *Funktion der Religion*, Frankfurt 1977

Harvey Cox, *The Secular City*, New York and London 1965

C.Torres, *Revolutionary Priest. Complete Writings*, London and New York 1971

G.Gutiérrez, *A Theology of Liberation*, Maryknoll 1973 and London 1974, ²1988

P.Freire, *The Pedagogy of the Oppressed*, London and New York 1972

H.Zwiefelhofer, *Neue Weltwirtschaftsordnung und katholische Soziallehre*, Munich 1980

J.H.Cone, *Black Theology and Black Power*, New York 1969

G.S.Wilmore and J.H.Cone, *Black Theology. A Documentary History 1966-1979*, New York 1979

M.Daly, *Beyond God the Father*, New York 1973 and London 1985

E.Moltmann-Wendel, *Menschenrechte für die Frau*, Munich 1973

R.R.Ruether, *Womenguides. Readings towards a Feminist Theology*, Boston 1985

P.Teilhard de Chardin, *The Phenomenon of Man*, London and New York 1959

id., *The Future of Man*, London and New York 1964

E.Bloch, *The Principle of Hope*, Oxford 1986

J.Moltmann, *Theology of Hope*, London and New York 1967

Chapter 4: Christian identity

K.Barth, *Church Dogmatics*, I.1-IV.4, Edinburgh 1936ff.

K.Rahner, *Foundations of Christian Faith*, New York and London 1978

A.Loisy, *The Gospel and the Church*, London 1903

J-.M.Lagrange, *L'Évangile de Jésus-Christ*, Paris 1928

A.Schweitzer, *The Quest of the Historical Jesus*, London and New York

A.von Harnack, *Marcion. Das Evangelium vom fremden Gott*, Leipzig 1924

C.Thoma, *Christliche Theologie des Judentums*, Aschaffenburg 1978

F.Mussner, *Traktat über die Juden*, Munich 1979

G. von Rad, *Old Testament Theology*, Edinburgh I, 1962; II, 1965, reissued London 1975

J.Moltmann, *The Church in the Power of the Spirit*, London and New York 1977

K.Adam, *The Son of God*, New York 1934

W.Pannenberg, *Jesus – God and Man*, Philadelphia and London 1968

W.Kasper, *Jesus the Christ*, London 1976

B.Forte, *Geschichte Gottes – Gott der Geschichte*, Mainz 1984

J.Sobrino, *Christology at the Crossroads. A Latin American Approach*, New York and London 1978

H.U von Balthasar, 'Mysterium Paschale', in *Mysterium Salutis. Grundriss heilsgeschichtlicher Dogmatik*, III.2, Einsiedeln 1969, 133-326

H.Mühlen, *Die Veränderlichkeit Gottes als Horizont einer zukünftigen Christologie*, Münster 1969

J.Moltmann, *The Crucified God*, London and New York 1974

E.Jüngel, *God as the Mystery of the World*, Grand Rapids and Edinburgh 1983

Chapter 5: Theology in an ecumenical age

R.Rouse and S.Neill, *A History of the Ecumenical Movement* (London and Philadelphia 1954), Geneva [3]1986

L.Vischer (ed.), *Die Einheit der Kirche*, Munich 1965

P.Abrecht (ed.), *Die Kirche als Faktor einer kommender Weltgemeinschaft*, Stuttgart 1966

E.Lange, *Die ökumenische Utopie oder Was bewegt die ökumenische Bewegung?*, Stuttgart 1972

W.Huber and H.E.Tödt, *Menschenrechte. Perspektiven einer menschlichen Welt*, Stuttgart 1977

J.Lochman and J.Moltmann, *Gottes Recht und Menschenrechte*, Neukirchen-Vluyn 1977

Papal Commission 'Iustitia et pax', *The Church and Human Rights*, Rome 1975

II

Mediating Theology Today

In historical terms, any Christian theology is a 'mediating theology' whether or not it is aware of the fact, since it mediates the Christian message that has been handed down in such a way that it falls within the horizons of the understanding of the people of a particular time. Mediation between the Christian tradition and the culture of the present is the most important task of theology. Without a living relationship to the possibilities and problems of the man or woman of the present, Christian theology becomes sterile and irrelevant. But without reference to the Christian tradition Christian theology becomes opportunist and uncritical. Historical mediation must both work to achieve the true preservation of the identity of the Christian message and see that it is relevant to the present. Christian theology has succeeded in making great syntheses in its history. For centuries the theology of the early church was a successful and well-tried synthesis between Christian tradition and Hellenistic culture. While the Reformation again concentrated entirely on the identity of the biblical Christian proclamation, it became effective in culture only as a result of the Protestant humanism of Melanchthon and Calvin, which has shaped the modern world in Western and Central Europe. However, so far Christian theology has not yet succeeded in arriving at a single, generally convincing, synthesis in the perspective of modern culture. The phenomenon of 'modernity' is too unclear and too varied. The modern spirit questions each tradition and especially each religious tradition too critically, and relativizes it. So in the face of the specific problems of this modern world the mediating theology of the Christian tradition has a twofold task. On the one hand it must defend the right and the significance of Christian faith against the doubt and the criticism of the modern spirit *apologetically*. On the other hand it must show that the Christian faith has therapeutic relevance to the sicknesses of the modern spirit and the perplexities of the modern world. The present-day mediation of Christian faith to the modern world is always determined by apologetic interests on the one hand and by interests which are critical of culture and therapeutic on the other. That distinguishes modern 'mediating theology' from its predecessors in the pre-modern eras.

The phenomenon of the modern world is many-sided, and the interpretations which it gives of itself are equally so; the theological points of contact for the communication of the Christian tradition are correspondingly numerous. Those who compare the modern world world principally with the integrally Christian culture of the 'Holy Roman Empire' in the Middle Ages say that the modern world is a 'secular world'. Others who compare the modern world with the cosmocentricity of earlier periods say that it owes itself to the 'anthropocentric shift' in the Renaissance and Reformation. And those who demonstrate how the old orientation of human culture on the world of nature has given way to the new orientation of human culture on world history and its progress say that the modern world is a 'historical world'.

The modern world is in fact a unique 'experiment'. It is the first 'project' of humankind which has been created for human ends and with human means. 'Scientific-technological civiliz-

54

ation' is now becoming increasingly the destiny of all human-kind. It is spreading irresistibly in countries which are consequently called 'developing countries'. It is inexorably being developed further. Not least, sociology shows with hard facts and data that the old agrarian society which was friendly towards nature is being replaced by industrial society which exploits nature and is concerned only with human ends. A century ago the majority of people live in the country. Today the majority of people live in the major conurbations. The great trek from the country to the cities is going on, and today also determines the situation of peoples in the Third World: 'The technological house, the technological city, the earth which is dominated by the technological city and is made the house of humankind – that is the symbol of the age, the age of the fulfilment of technological utopia, the age of the inhabitation of the earth by humankind and the appropriation and trans-formation of the earth by humankind.'[1] Thus in practice secular-ization means urbanization and industrialization. Historiciz-ation means the programmed progress of the development of industrial power.

The phenomenon of this 'modern world' is in fact unique in human history. For the first time a human world made by human beings is detaching itself from the world of nature. Orientation on the laws and rhythms of nature is overlaid by orientation on hopes and aims which men and women set themselves. People no longer want to 'live in accordance with nature', as was said in antiquity and in Asian societies; they want to construct reality in accordance with their own concep-tions and projects. Human destiny is no longer determined by the powers of nature but by the human will. Modern men and women are therefore no longer primarily terrified by natural catastrophes, but by the great human atrocities like Auschwitz, Hiroshima and the possible future nuclear destruction of the world. Does 'God' still have a place and a function in this world, which is increasingly becoming the world of humankind? What is the significance of 'faith' in this world of human power and human responibility? What social and political role can the 'churches' play as they disappear in great cities between apartment blocks, hotel palaces and skyscrapers? It is understandable – though not Christian – that often the first reaction of the churches to this unprecedented 'new world' has been one of apocalyptic anxiety, and they have condemned it as the 'apostasy of faith' into godlessness, as anti-Christian rebellion against God and as the beginning of the universal downfall of the world. The various churches have varied greatly in the time they have taken to respond to the new situation of men and women in the modern world: first in the seventeenth century were the Protestant Free Churches of the Baptists and Methodists in England, and then in the age of the Enlightenment the Protestant churches on the continent. In the Second Vatican Council the Roman Catholic Church achieved its great *aggiornamento* to modern times. The Orthodox Churches still have to undergo this process of transformation and adapation. On the other hand, the modern world itself began with fundamental breaks in tradition, in order to make a radical prescription for its own progress. In the face of their tutelage under the powers of tradition and the church, modern men and women gained their freedom through resolute emancipation, by displacing the past which had become alien and orientating themselves on their own future. At all events, they said, the past is a prologue to the future. Atheism, rather than belief in God, was made the guarantee of their personal and social freedom. If there is a God, then men and women are not free. But they must be free and responsible for this world, therefore there may not be a God.[2] In this situation between the apocalyptic conservatism of the churches and many believers and the optimistic belief in progress held by modern freedom-loving men and women, to engage in mediating theology is not a peaceful but a controversial task.

As examples I shall take four great attempts at mediation here, using them to describe the problems of theology in the modern world:

1. Existential theology: Rudolf Bultmann and the problem of history.

2. Transcendental theology: Karl Rahner and the problem of anthropocentricity.

3. Cultural theology: Paul Tillich and the religious interpretation of the secular world.

4. Political theology and imperfect modernity.

1. Existentialist theology: Rudolf Bultmann and the problem of history

Historical criticism is the most serious crisis for Christian faith and it has not yet been overcome. The age of the Enlightenment began in the seventeenth century with the historical criticism of traditions and legends about rule in church and state. The unmasking of the 'Donation of Constantine' as a legend of the foundation of the church-state was only the begining. Historical-critical biblical scholarship was developed within Protestantism, and from the time of Johann Salomo Semler it became the expression of the intellectual honesty of the educated man in Europe.[3] The object of its criticism was the doctrine of the verbal inspiration of 'Holy Scripture', which had declared scripture to be infallible, self-sufficient, free of contradiction and thus the absolute authority in all questions of faith and life. In the Catholic sphere the assertion of the infallibility of the church's *magisterium* a hundred years later was shown with equal incorruptibility and impartiality to be historically conditioned, and was questioned by the critics. In the bourgeois world the historical-critical approach to religious authority in the Bible and the church was – and indeed still is – regarded as the foundation for its religious freedom.[4] But this approach also led to the inescapable recognition of the historical relativity of all the values and ideas which humankind has held, and continues to hold, to be holy, absolute or divine. Historical relativism, for which there can be no absolutes in history other than the universal relativity of all things, was the consequence of historical criticism. But in that case how can faith, which is unconditional certainty, ground itself in historical tradition, which is always relative, is based only on probabilities, and is handed down in so uncertain a way?[5] How can faith in God, which is both absolute and necessary, rest on chance historical events? G.E.Lessing had already declared in the eighteenth century that 'accidental truths of history can never become the proof of necessary truths of reason'.[6] The development of the historical-critical consciousness removed the ground not only from under religious authorities, but also from under all values and norms in the ethos of society. Historical relativism led to the subjectivism of the modern pluralistic society. For the inner motivation of historical-critical research was the liberation of present-day men and women from the tutelage of the traditions. 'The historical consciousness breaks the last chains which philosophy and natural science were unable to break. Mankind is now completely free.'[7] The 'historical investigation of a human pattern of thought always serves to free us from it'.[8] 'The true criticism of dogma is its history.'[9]

But in what does this freedom of the present from the pressure of past tradition consist? Does it not lead to a new absolutism of the present over against the past? If historical consciousness communicates insight into the temporal relativity of all things, then the present itself is also relative, and 'everything is in process, in flux, and nothing abides' (W.Dilthey). 'The history of the world as judgment on the

58

world shows every metaphysical system to be relative, provisional and transitory.' The problem of 'mediation' between Christian tradition and the secular present thus becomes insoluble. Ernst Troeltsch saw this most clearly, and was broken by it: it was no longer possible to make a positive synthesis of 'the relationship between the endless movement of the historical life-stream and the need of the human spirit to limit it and shape it by fixed norms', because the contradiction remains that 'one cannot speak of an absolute religion before the end of history'.[10]

Modern, liberal Protestantism was the first to look for a new answer to this challenge of the modern spirit. The development of the 'doctrine of faith' by Friedrich Schleiermacher lastingly shaped the Protestantism of the nineteenth century.[11] Schleiermacher replaced the church's christological dogma with the earthly Jesus who can be known through history, who through his 'ever-powerful consciousness of God' exerts redemptive influence on human consciousness of God which has been impaired by sin. Through his inner personality Jesus influenced and continues to influence human beings, in their 'immediate self-awareness', their souls, their consciences. Therefore he can be called the 'productive original' of the human being reconciled and united with God. Christianity is consequently a personal 'religion of redemption'. By going back to Jesus himself with reference to the history of christological dogma and putting Jesus' inner sinlessness and ever-powerful consciousness of God at the centre of his history rather than the supernatural incarnation and eschatological resurrection, Schleiermacher came to terms with historical criticism and accepted the anthropological shift of modern times: God is not present in objective historical facts but in the subjective consciousness of historical human beings. On the other hand he freed faith from dogmatic assertions and moral postulates and seated it in the human heart as the indwelling 'feeling of absolute dependence' on God. This solution was regarded for over a century as a brilliant one, because it removed the 'inner life' of Jesus and similarly the 'inner life' of the believer from the criticism of the modern historical and scientific consciousness. However, in turn it deprives Christianity of the possibility of criticizing the modern consciousness.

At the beginning of the twentieth century the Marburg theologian Wilhelm Herrmann (1846-1922) presented this solution to the modern spirit, sharpened by historical positivism and abroad scientific training.[12] For him knowledge of God was 'the defenceless expression of religious experience'. It was defenceless because it did not have the power of objective proofs; it was an expression because it was utterly related to this inner human experience. For Herrmann the world split into two different realities: the 'world of things' which could be explained, imagined, and brought under general concepts, and the world of selfhood, which could be experienced and expressed, and was accessible only to the individual. Neither God, the Absolute, nor the inner self of the human being, the central element, are to be found in the 'explainable world' of things. 'God' therefore cannot be 'proved' any more than inner experience can be proved. 'A God who can be proved is world, and a God who is world is an idol.'[13] Scientific psychology can dissolve the soul into a foreseeable mass of relations, but the unity in which we sum up the multiplicity of our inner states, our self-awareness, is something quite different from the knowledge of those relationships. By means of these distinctions, at a time when the riddle of the world was being taken apart by scientists and the consciousness illuminated by psychoanalysts, Herrmann attained another realm which was untouched by all this. 'God and the soul', or in modern terminology 'transcendence and existence',[14] do not belong in the objective world of proofs and criticism, but in the non-objective dimension of direct, inner experience. This is the subjective sphere of 'religion'. 'Religion is the awakening of the individual to an awareness of such a personal life grounded in itself.'[15] Here Christian theology renounces objective proofs of God from the world and from history. By relating God solely to the inner self-experience of human beings, however, it actually makes a virtue of this modern crisis over proof. Religious self-experience is the basis for the inner personality of human beings; it gives stability to their souls and is the basis for their sovereign freedom over against the world. Not only is God no longer to be found in the modern mechanistic view of the world and in the modern world of institutions and machines; even human personality vanishes. The human being becomes either a nexus of social roles, a robot, or a 'Man without Qualities', to use the title of Robert Musil's novel. Religion, however – understood as subjective faith – rescues the destroyed subjectivity of those who live in the mass conurbations of modern civilization and makes personalities out of adapted objects. The apologetic and critical-therapeutic sides of this modern 'mediating theology' can be seen clearly.

Rudolf Bultmann (1884-1976) was a New Testament scholar and at the same time one of the most influential theologians of the twentieth century.[16] In his historical study of the New Testament he was particularly exposed to – and indebted to – the historical-critical consciousness. As a loyal pupil of Wilhelm Herrmann in Marburg Bultmann knew Hermann's Protestant 'theology of mediation'. As a result of his later friendship with Martin Heidegger, he came to use the terminology of existentialist philosophy, but his basic theological ideas had been fixed before that. In 1920 he wrote very much along the lines of Wilhelm Herrmann: 'Of course religion is a private matter and has nothing to do with the state.'[17] It is an individual matter which has nothing to do with what is general. So religion does not have any 'history' either: at all times it knows of only one problem, which must always be solved anew and always

61

in terms of the individual: 'Finding the power over against which free self-surrender is possible.'[18] This power is God as the 'all-determining reality' which all individuals can perceive personally in their inner experience of themselves, in so far as they entrust themselves to God. To speak of God apart from this inner self-experience is abstraction and blasphemy. One can only speak of God out of inner involvement. To speak of God is at the same time to speak of one's own existence.[19] Any statement about God is at the same time a statement about one's own existence. Theology is at the same time anthropology, and vice versa.

Bultmann used the term 'existence' as early as 1921, but he meant by it what Kierkegaard meant when he used the term 'self' and what Augustine meant when he used the term 'soul'. Existence is an individual's 'capacity for being a self' (Heidegger). With the help of Heidegger's existentialist analysis, Bultmann extended these old concepts and developed as basic conditions of human existence the existentialia of historicity, temporality, resolution and futurity and the categories of authentic and inauthentic existence. With a clear cultural criticism he demarcated his anthropology from human society and the cosmos of nature; authentic human community is limited to the personal I-Thou relationship. By contrast, in institutionalized society individuals lose themselves, play only a social role, wear only a prefabricated mask and live among inessentials. For Bultmann these are the distinguishing marks of the large city ('The large cities are not true...') and the modern social state which turns the human virtues of giving and receiving into claims and achievements: 'Where mutual relationship is arranged by organization, trust ceases to be the bond between one person and another.'[20] Nature also vanishes from sight along with society, and the existential corporeality of human beings is displaced into inauthenticity along with the natural environment. Modern Christian theology is like an ellipse with two foci: God and the real self or existence or soul. For its task is to make it clear that faith does not seek any supports within the world nor any certainties within the world, but conveys pure, personal trust in the God who is not an object and with that freedom from this world.

The exegetical and hermeneutical programmes for which Bultmann has become famous, the programmes of demythologizing and the existentialist interpretation of the Christian tradition, follow from this basic idea of 'God and existence'.[21] Exegesis is to do with texts which come from history. Exegetes themselves stand in history, i.e. exist historically, and are motivated by questions about themselves in specific historical experiences and decisions. These shape their pre-understanding, their preliminary attitude to the content which is expressed in the text. If we take account of both these facts, then any interpretation of historical texts must be a historical, i.e. existential, interpretation, because otherwise it fails to do justice to the intention of the historical texts. Historical texts were written by historical people. In them these historical figures express their historical self-understanding directly or indirectly. Religious historical texts express this self-understanding in connection with the experience of God of a particular time. If we were only to consider them objectively and observe them neutrally, then we would set them above history and would not understand anything. Perception of their distinctive historical existence is part of the historical understanding of the texts of the tradition. Only when we are moved by the questions of our own historical existence will we understand the historical texts. In that case our question will no longer be historical and objective ('What did these texts mean in their time?') but existential ('What do these texts mean for me today?').

Any exegesis of historical texts is at the same time the exegetes' exegesis of themselves. Conversely, one comes to interpret one's own existence by coming to terms with the texts of past historical existence. Bultmann began with the thesis that the interpretation of history is the interpretation of the self and the interpretation of the self takes place in the interpretation of history.[22] The hermeneutics of historical texts always takes place within the framework of the hermeneutical structure of human existence, for human beings tend historically towards self-understanding and self-interpretation and are directed towards it. Therefore in Bultmann's hermeneutical theology exegesis and theology, or historical and systematic theology, coincide; here the present always has the priority, for 'history is a call to historicity'.[23] This is the basic notion of existentialist interpretation.

The programme of the 'demythologization' of the Christian message handed down in the New Testament, which Bultmann published in 1941 and which became probably the most controversial theological programme of the twentieth century, arose out of this with an inner logic. Bultmann begins from the fact that compared with the modern world-view of science and technology the way in which the New Testament writings understand the world is a mythological one. The conception of the three-storey world – heaven, earth, hell – is mythological; the expectation that supernatural powers intervene in the natural course of things is mythological; the apocalyptic expectation of an imminent end to the world is mythological. 'We cannot use electric lights and radios and, in the event of illness, avail ourselves of modern medical and clinical means and at the same time believe in the spirit and wonder world of the New Testament.'[24] Anyone nowadays who called for the acceptance of the biblical world-view would compel the believer to make a *sacrificium intellectus* and degrade faith into superstition. The Christian message is not about the world-view of New Testament times but about the experience of God in the self-understanding of faith. Therefore the biblical message –

64

the call of that history – must be detached from the mythical world-view and translated into our present-day understanding of existence. In negative terms, the New Testament message must be demythologized; in positive terms, this message must be interpreted in existentialist terms.

It is quite clear that Bultmann is not involved in a reduction of the Christian message but with its necessary translation, though this is often misunderstood.[25] Is he successful in this? This is disputed, because Bultmann uses too narrow a concept of myth when he says that myth is 'the objectifying expression of existential experiences'. Myth always at the same time tells stories of origins. Bultmann did not take up the concept of myth that is to be found in Durkheim's and Malinowski's sociology of religion. Moreover, his starting point is that the New Testament kerygma is essentially existential address, a call to the decision of faith. This definition too is too narrow, since it does not take note of the narrative accounts of the gospel, e.g. in the eucharistic tradition. Finally, his understanding of faith is one-sidedly related to the present historicity of existence. It omits to note that concrete historicity is always disclosed, made possible and limited through history that really happened, and not vice versa. The history of Jesus Christ is not an expression of faith; rather, its impact on men and women calls forth faith. Therefore the history of Christ precedes the historicity of faith, and faith owes itself to that history. Even if the basis of Christian faith only discloses itself to the believer, in content it precedes the origin of faith and does not coincide with it.

After Bultmann the discussion of this hermeneutical theology of mediation has taken different directions, but its task and its possibility are generally recognized. First of all Bultmann's world-view proved inadequate.[26] He began from the domination of the principle of causality in the mechanistic world-view of the modern sciences. He did not note the

65

development of new quantum physics and the biological theory of open life-systems. The bisection of the world undertaken by W.Herrmann for apologetic reasons, into the 'explainable world of things' and the 'experienceable world of selfhood', the old dichotomy between objectivity and subjectivity, is now no longer scientifically, anthropologically or personally tenable; the world-view of modern science is essentially more open than Bultmann assumed. Existentialist interpretation also proved too narrow. In Heidegger and Bultmann it was bound up with a romantic cultural criticism of modern society and was addressed only to the cultured classes, for whom 'existence' was experience of the self and not economic, social and political survival. Consequently in 1968 the programme of the existentialist interpretation of the Christian message was taken up by the programme of political theology[27] and the materialist exegesis of the theology of liberation[28] and superseded. The biblical message of God is addressed to all of life and all of reality, since God is 'the all-determining reality' (Bultmann). It cannot be limited to the private inwardness of the believer, to the purely religious dimension of life or to the community within the church. It unavoidably has political dimensions and indisputably has cosmic horizons. Discussion of hermeneutics after Bultmann has also burst the narrow limits of his existentialist interpretation.

More recent 'narrative theology' has rediscovered the significance of the narrative parts of the Old and New Testaments as well as their kerygmatic and appellative forms of speech. More recent linguistic hermeneutics has introduced the sociology of language to biblical hermeneutics and burst open its personalistic narrowness. Finally, the beginnings of a structuralist exegesis have done away with the anthropocentric one-sidedness in existentialist hermeneutics. Bultmann's programmatic theology has been influential not so much in its positive effects as in its challenge to produce a relevant

66

mediation of the original Christian message to the modern world, and it continues to have an effect today far beyond confessional limits.

2. Transcendental theology: Karl Rahner and the problem of anthropocentricity

The modern European world arose out of the so-called 'anthropocentric shift'. The ancient world in which Plato and Aristotle lived and thought was a cosmocentric world. The individual understood himself as a member of his human society, and the human society (*polis*) understood itself as a part of the divine cosmos of the natural order. The mediaeval world in which Anselm of Canterbury and Thomas Aquinas lived and thought was a theocentric world. Man and nature, society and cosmos were ordered around God, the absolute and perfect Being. With the beginning of modern times in the Renaissance, Reformation and Enlightenment, however, man increasingly made himself the measure of all things and the centre of the world, since through his sciences and technologies he increasingly made this natural world his own. Science and technology make him the 'Lord and possessor of nature'.[29] He becomes its subject, and it becomes his object. The world of nature is de-divinized, secularized and made the material of human will. Human beings lose their corporeality and are understood only as that subject of knowledge and will which can set itself over against nature and its own corporeality. The modern 'metaphysics of subjectivity', which was first formulated by Descartes when he distinguished between the *res cogitans* and the *res extensa* and defined them in relation to each other, still dominates Western philosophy and is simply the ontological basis of the 'planetary imperialism of technologically organized man'.[30] The world of nature which surrounds and supports humankind is conceived of in a world-view and in this view is produced according to human standards. Thus the question of the nature and determination of human beings comes to the centre of all sciences. The interpretation of the world is rooted in anthropology, since human beings judge all things by their criterion.

But this makes our questions about ourselves, our true being and our historical determination impossible to answer. Nature, in subjection, can no longer give a reply. Heaven, denied, keeps silence. Modern men and women are detached from their original integration into nature and religion. So they find themselves with a permanent identity crisis. 'What is man?' is their central question, and no one can answer it for them, least of all those who raise the question.[31] It was only logical that Immanuel Kant should have formulated the basic questions of modern philosophy as he did. He answered the question 'What can I know?' in his *Critique of Pure Reason*; he answered the question 'What shall I do?' in his *Critique of Practical Reason*; and he answered the question 'What may I hope for?' in his *Religion within the Limits of Reason Alone*. But when it came to the question 'What is man?', Kant said: 'Basically one could count all this as anthropology, because the first three questions relate to the last.'[32] However, he was not in a position to answer the question. He never wrote an *Anthropology* to match. Up until Heidegger no one answered this fourth question, the answer to which was meant to solve all the other questions, and even he could only answer it only by shifting it to the question of 'being' itself.[33]

In accordance with this 'shift', modern religion is anthropo-centric and subject-orientated. The centre is occupied not by God, but by the consciousness of God; not by the history of Christ but by the historicity of the believer; not by objective belief, but by subjective believing. This shift to the subjective meaning of faith already began in the Reformation. People no longer asked 'What is that?' but 'What does it mean for me?'[34]

68

Of course this also opened up the way for the criticism of religion. If everything religious is related to a human subject, then this subject can also be made the measure of all religious things. 'Anthropology' was discovered and revealed as the mystery of theology (Feuerbach). It was not God who created man in his image but man who creates gods as he desires.[35] 'Religion is the self-awareness of the man who has either not yet achieved himself or has already lost himself again. Religion is the illusory sun which revolves round human beings as long as they do not move round themselves… To be radical is to get to the root of things. For man, the root is man himself.'[36]

Under these anthropocentric conditions of modern times Christian theology can become credible only as 'anthropo-theology'.[37] It must accept the changed conditions and in them express Christian belief in God. Karl Rahner (1904-1984) has become normative here in the sphere of Catholic theology and far beyond its bounds with his transcendental theology.[38] Of course his theology is shaped by the kindred transcendental philosophy of German Idealism, but in content it is merely meant to be a reflective understanding of what had always already been a theme of Christian tradition, namely God's communication of himself to the human subject. If the human subject is destined to receive God's communication of himself, then it has transcendence in its make-up. God's communication of himself to humankind through grace is matched by the fundamental inner self-transcendence of the human being. Therefore transcendental theology clarifies the 'a priori conditions in the believing subject for the knowledge of any truth of faith'.[39]

So, like Bultmann, Rahner develops the old theme of Augustinian theology, 'God and the soul', and transfers it to modern men and women, who have become questions which they themselves cannot answer. With his concentration on the subjective inwardness of the experience of the self and God,

Rahner can overcome the offence caused to modern intellects by dogmatic faith and faith in the so-called saving facts. 'The significance in terms of concrete living of historical facts is something which man is quite incapable of rendering intelligible without transcendental theology.'[40] He makes the inner identity crisis experienced by modern men and women more profound by making more profound their unanswerable question about themselves in a mystical way, so that it becomes that mystery which is the innermost part of our being, in which we touch on the mystery that is called 'God'. Modern men and women, who falsely seek salvation in objective truths and achievements, must first be shown the objective impossibility of disclosing his existence, i.e. clarifying their inner 'mystery'. Because by virtue of their self-transcendence human beings are made for God, only God's disclosure of himself can fulfil human existence. Rahner must therefore show that the divine truth of Christianity is related to the subject and has a subjective character. For modern men and women it enters the dimension of the 'mystical', the 'mystery', the 'paradox'. 'Subjectivity', undemonstrable but inescapable, 'is truth'.[41]

Karl Rahner's theology has two dimensions, an inner one and an outer one: the mysticism of the *Exercises* of Ignatius of Loyola and apologetic addressed to the modern world which has become anthropocentric. His theology has rightly been called a 'modern translation of mystical experience'. Here I shall take up his striking comments on 'anonymous Christians' from his work, using them to demonstrate the patterns of thought in the mediation of transcendental theology.[42]

In modern society the Christian church has got itself into an apparently insoluble dilemma: how can the Christian claim of universal salvation ('God wills all people to be saved', I Tim.2.4) be presented by a church which is increasingly becoming a minority in a world of religious pluralism? Must one not assume that there must also be 'anonymous Christians' outside the church? What is the relationship between being a Christian and being truly human, between being truly human and being Christian? Does not the particular reality of faith presuppose its own universal possibility and by that demonstrate its claim to truth? Rahner answers with a modern translation of the mediaeval schema of 'nature and grace'. Just as grace presupposes nature and does not destroy it but perfects it, so God presupposes the free and gracious communication of creation to itself, and communicates himself to it with the possibility of accepting the divine self-communication. Human beings have the inner capacity to perceive and accept God's approach in his revelation. In so far as God is the infinite, incomprehensible and hidden one, in this respect men and women must be called 'beings of unlimited openness for the limitless being of God'.[43] His transcendental openness is 'an indefinability come to consciousness of itself';[44] in theological terms this means that such a person is directed towards the infinite mystery, God. The 'mystery' of being human is the mystery of the infinite God and vice versa. Anthropology and theology are therefore indissolubly in a correlative relationship to each other. From God's side this necessitates the theological statement that man is the being which arises when God communicates himself in the incarnation. From the human side this necessitates the anthropological statement that man is the being who comes to himself when he surrender himself to the incomprehensible mystery of God. This universal human self-transcendence which is part of human nature therefore achieves its true completion and fulfilment in God's communication of himself in Christ. In this respect the incarnation of God is the 'unique, *supreme* case of the total actualization of human reality'.[45] The immanence of God in humankind and the transcendence of humankind in God coincide in Christ.

Rahner can also relate these two sides to each other as 'inward and outward', as 'anonymous and explicit', and say that in the experience of their transcendence, human beings also already experience an offer of divine grace. 'The revelation of the word in Christ... is only the possibility of expressing what we already are by grace.' It follows from this that 'the expressly Christian revelation becomes the explicit statement of the revelation in grace which man experiences explicitly in the depths of his being'.[46] God's communication of himself which is offered to all human beings in Christ is the 'goal of creation' and fulfils creation. Therefore, Rahner concludes with a bold turn of thought, on the one hand to be a Christian simply amounts to being truly and expressly human, and to be truly human already amounts to being an 'anonymous' Christian. The one who comes to his being and achieves his true being is a Christian, whether he knows it or not, for 'he also already accepts this revelation if he really accepts himself *completely*, for it already speaks in him.'[47] 'He takes upon himself in that Yes to himself the grace of the mystery which has radically approached us',[48] and it is that to which we give the name 'God'.

Rahner therefore establishes the universal claim of Christianity by showing that to be a Christian is to be 'explicitly human' and that to be truly human is to be an 'anonymous' Christian. He describes human selfhood and the being of God as a 'mystery'. By that he means both that it cannot be defined and that it cannot be fathomed. One can solve riddles, but mysteries must be respected and revered in silence. By transcending all known definitions and names of God and humanity and pointing to the ever greater impossibility of defining and giving names, he achieves the possibility of a universal assent to his theological statements, since assent is easier to achieve in undefinable negatives than with definitions in positive statements. Greater communion arises in the silence before the infinite unfathomable mystery than in the statement which all too quickly attracts counter-statements. With his thesis of the 'anonymous Christian' Rahner opens up the bounds of the church for men and women in the modern world. He overcomes the church's sectarian retreat into itself. But of course he defines 'true humanity' in terms of being Christian. If true humanity is 'anonymous Christianity', then on the other hand being a Christian is 'explicit humanity' and thus also its criterion. So while Rahner may clarify the universal significance of being a Christian in particular, does he also take seriously the pluralism of religions and the freedom of religion in the modern world? Is not too much being asked of Christian existence if it is already meant to depict the universal truth of humanity? Is that not the old claim to absoluteness on which so many Christians have come to grief and in which the church too is made painfully aware of its imperfection? Do we not also have Jewish existence and human existence in other religions alongside Christian existence, each its own way of being 'expressly human'?

Like Bultmann, Rahner raises with great openness the claim of modern men and women to 'intellectual honesty'. At the beginning of the Enlightenment G.E.Lessing had said critically that 'accidental truths of history can never become the proof of necessary truths of reason'. Rahner takes up this reproof. It is 'no longer a simple matter for modern man to accept as worthy of faith the position that the event of the incarnation should have taken place just once'.[49] So he enquires into what is universal in that unique historical event and develops his theory of human beings as the 'idea of Christ'.[50] What corresponds to the accidental history of Christ in the inner subjectivity of every human being? It is the 'idea of Christ', namely the prior openness of human beings to the appearance of the incarnate God. What has happened outwardly in that history finds a parallel and an echo in our inner experience. The 'idea of Christ' arises in human beings in so far as they look towards the supreme and at the same time free fulfilment of their being.

Rahner discovers in inner human self-transcendence a kind of 'anonymous' or 'seeking christology'. Unless there were this idea of Christ in the human make-up, then no one would be in a position to recognize Jesus as the Christ and believe in him. To presuppose this idea of Christ in every human being is the basic presupposition of any Christian theology, for the mystery manifest in Christ is also the mystery of creation. All human nature is directed towards grace, because grace presupposes this nature. Therefore Rahner describes christology as 'self-transcending anthropology' and anthropology as 'deficient christology'.[51] Human beings are 'themselves a mystery, always far beyond themselves into the mystery of God', and Jesus, the God-man, communicates his mystery to us by participating in our being. His mystery consists in the nameless, infinite, inexhaustibly spendthrift love of God. We participate in it in so far as we find in his mystery the power in the face of which free self-surrender is possible for us. Thus 'experience from within and the message from without come to meet each other'.[52] This correspondence can also be seen in Jesus himself; on the one hand Jesus is the man 'whose life is one of absolutely unique self-surrender to God';[53] on the other hand this surrender of human beings to God implies 'God's absolute communication of himself' to human beings.

The 'christology from above' which begins from the incarnation of God exactly matches the 'christology from below' which begins from consciousness of God and Jesus' surrender to God. The human being who makes himself over to God and the God who empties himself in humanity are one in the God-man Jesus Christ. Rahner then goes on to find precisely this divine-human structure in the relationship between christology and anthropology: Christ is not only the descent of God but also the ascent and the future of humankind. The incarnation of God and man is simultaneously the climax of the history of salvation and of evolution. By accepting the basic ideas of modern evolutionary theories Rahner – unlike Bultmann – extends his anthropology by cosmology. 'Self-transcendence' is one of the structural principles of the self-organization of matter and open life-systems. The course of evolution which transcends itself leads from matter to life, to consciousness, to spirit. As spiritual beings, men and women can be understood as the 'self-transcendence of living matter'.[54] Interpreted theologically, human self-transcendence extends to the mystery of God and is directed towards the Christ event in which surrender to God and God's communication of himself take place. Seen from this goal, the goal of evolution then becomes God's communication of himself in the world.[55] On the basis of this world-view Rahner has proclaimed God as 'the absolute future' in many conversations with Marxists and scientists, and has related all relative futures of human aims and hopes to the mystery of this absolute future. Christian theology does not know more of the future than other sciences and ideologies, but less, because it sees the 'absolute future' of the world as God's mystery, and learns to honour it by criticism of utopias and ideologies.

The strength of Rahner's theory of mediation to the world which has become anthropocentric and to the unfathomable subjectivity of modern men and women lies in the fact that it mediates the whole Christian tradition, abandoning nothing, and that it does so by stressing the meaning of the mystical dimension of the depths of Christian faith, not mediating it cheaply. However, the strength of Rahner's position is also its weakness. In the face of the justified critical question of the modern spirit about the mediaeval form of Christianity, must there not be not only mediations but also revisions of the Christian tradition? The theory of the 'anonymous Christian' outside the Christian church could also have the hidden purpose of laying claim to all that is truly human through the church. Humanists who have spoken out against the

75

Christianity that they know may not perhaps want to be termed 'anonymous Christians', any more than believing Christians might want to be called 'anonymous Buddhists'. Can one be a Christian 'anonymously', without mentioning and confessing the name of Christ? Is to be a Christian explicitly already to be truly human? Were that the case, then being a Christian would indeed have a universal significance and also make a universal claim on all that is truly human. But that would not allay the suspicion that this inclusive openness in being a Christian to all that is truly human is simply a matter of advancing in a different form the old claim of the church to rule the world. In the history of God with humankind is not Jewish existence also a witness to God's righteousness and future alongside Christian existence? And therefore must not the church of Christ for theological reasons first recognize Israel as God's people alongside itself in the salvation history of the world? In that case, may it call believing and righteous Jews 'anonymous Christians'?

I do not think that this is possible. Therefore I would suggest that we need more distinctions in talk about being Christian and being human, about church and world. It might even meet Rahner's concern if we first stressed more strongly the eschatological difference between the church of Christ and the kingdom of God, and between the present kingdom of grace and the future kingdom of the glory of God. The church is not yet the kingdom of God itself, but only the mediation, preparation and witness of the kingdom that is to come. In this way it discovers Israel alongside it as the other mediation, preparation and witness of the coming kingdom of God.[56] The coming kingdom of God is understood in accordance with the hope of prophets and apostles as the new creation in which God's righteousness dwells. Therefore according to this hope, humanity too will only be perfected in that new creation. The kingdom of God, too, is also the truly human kingdom of men and women, who are meet for God's presence. The kingdom of God is not least the kingdom of peace for all creation: 'There will be no suffering, no crying, and death will be no more...' (Rev.21.4). If that is the consummation, then it cannot be said that grace already perfects nature; rather, it prepares it for the glory to come and only 'perfects' it in this sense. In that case one cannot say, either, that the incarnation of God in Christ is the goal of creation: rather, the incarnation of Christ prepares for creation and for the cosmic indwelling of the glory of God and pefects creation in this sense. Being Christian is therefore to be seen as an anticipation of true humanity under the conditions of incomplete history and this unredeemed world. Being Christian is a 'way of God' to the goal of the consummation of the world.

Starting from Barth and Rahner, more recent theology with a stronger eschatological orientation has stressed these differences and directions particularly in respect of Israel. Building on Barth and Rahner, more recent theology with a political orientation has given those whom Rahner calls 'anonymous Christians' a specific name and discovered them in the 'poor, the hungry, the sick, the thirsty and the prisoners' of Matt.25 whom Christ calls the least of his brothers and sisters and in whom he will himself be present, in order to wait for the acts of the righteous: 'Whatever you have done for one of them you have done for me.' If Christ is himself present in them, the necessary consequence is the 'preferential option' of the church 'for the poor'. As a result of the support of the church for the poor, the poor are brought out of the anonymity into which they have been driven. For their part the poor bring believing Christians into the special fellowship with Christ in which the poor already live.

The urgent problem today is not so much the particularity of the church in modern pluralist society as the convincing support of the church for the poor and oppressed in this modern society. It is not the bourgeois liberalism in the First World which confronts theology with the fundamental problems of mediation and making present, but the liberation of the poor and dying in the Third World and among the displaced strata of modern society in the First World.

3. Cultural theology: Paul Tillich and the religious interpretation of the secular world

It was Paul Tillich (1886-1965) who more than any other contemporary theologian took on the task of 'mediating' the Christian message to the modern world. For this he developed a method of his own, the 'method of correlation'. His *Systematic Theology* (1951-1964) was based on this method, and the wealth of articles he wrote on the religious interpretation of culture, art, science and politics shows the fruitfulness of his approach.[57] Tillich accepts the secularization of the modern world. He affirms the autonomy of modern men and women. He rejects any clerical heteronomy and any Christian claim to rule. But he seeks to disclose to autonomous men and women the depths of the theonomy of their beings and to set free again the religious dimension of modern culture from its displacements and wrongful occupations. Although for Tillich theology is 'a function of the church', his theology is an authentic theology of culture, since for him the culture with which human beings respond to the questions of their basic situations at all times and in all places, by giving themselves forms of life, is the real vehicle of the religious and the most universal manifestation of the absolute: religion is the substance of culture – culture is the form of religion.

It is the task of the theologian to expound the truth of the Christian message and interpret it anew for each generation.[58] So theologians are caught in a tension between the eternal truth and the situation of the time in which this truth is to be

78

perceived. Conservatism is mistaken if it clings to supposedly 'timeless' truth, since this does not occur in time but always only as 'yesterday's truth', in the form in which it was understood and perceived by people in earlier times. Liberalism is mistaken if it surrenders the Christian identity and is concerned only with the religious questions of the present. The true task of theology lies in the correlation of tradition and situation, since theology is always 'answering theology': 'It answers the questions implied in the "situation" in the power of the eternal message and with the means provided by the situation whose questions it answers.'[59]

Tillich therefore criticizes both the 'theology of diastasis' that he thinks he can see in Karl Barth, and the 'theology of synthesis' as developed by E.Troeltsch. Between the two of these for him there is the living method of correlation, which relates message and situation in such a way that neither is impaired by the other, but the questions contained in the situation are related to the answers which are contained in the message and vice versa. Message and situation are interpreted reciprocally and so united in the living interplay of question and answer. But what 'questions of the situation' are dealt with in the theological correlation? These are not penultimate questions but only the ultimate question, not conditional questions but only the unconditional question, the 'existential question' about the ground of being and the meaning of life. If this question is worked out, one can see what God is answering in his historical revelation. According to Tillich the method of the correlation of mesage and situation is grounded in the ontological correlation between God and man: 'God answers man's questions, and under the impact of God's answers man asks them.'[60] Theology must therefore disclose the questions contained in human existence and formulate them with reference to God, and it must formulate the answers lying in the divine self-revelation in terms of the questions which lie in human existence. The unity of the two lies outside history. Therefore the historical task can never be finished. Existential questions are questions which concern the whole of human existence. 'Only those who have experienced the shock of transitoriness, the anxiety in which they are aware of their finitude, the threat of nonbeing, can understand what the notion of God means. Only those who have experienced the tragic ambiguities of our historical existence and have totally questioned the meaning of experience can understand what the symbol of the Kingdom of God means.'[61]

The existential question is not a question which human beings have or do not have: human beings are themselves this question, before they put it. Humanity is the question, and religions and cultures are the answers, which are historical and therefore always get out of date. Being human is existentially questionable because it is not based in itself but in another, and has alienated itself from this foundation. But where Being itself appears in human existence and human beings find their 'ultimate concern' and pursue it unconditionally, one can speak of the divine answer to the questionableness of being human. Tillich therefore formulates the object of theology, in the old 'God and the soul' tradition of Augustine, in the same way as Rahner and Bultmann. 'The object of theology is what concerns us ultimately. Only those propositions are theological which deal with their object in so far as it can become a matter of ultimate concern for us.'[62] Political, social and cultural issues whch concern us only conditionally, provisionally and relatively are excluded from this transcendental determination of theology. 'Theology should never leave the situation of ultimate concern and try to play a role within the arena of preliminary concerns.'[63] For 'what concerns us ultimately' decides our being or non-being.

In this way Tillich creates for himself a basis which he can use in fundamental theology and apologetic, by relating the specific history of God which has been handed down to the universal, religious and metaphysical dimension of human existence. He puts it in the category of 'what concerns us ultimately' and in so doing takes up Luther's exposition of the First Commandment which says: 'The trust and faith of the heart makes both God and idol... for the two belong together, God and faith. That on which you set your heart and rely is really your God.'[64] What concerns a person ultimately becomes his or her God or idol. 'God' is the answer to the question which lies in human finitude and is the name for that which concerns us ultimately. This place can also be occupied, however, by idols and idolized finitudes like money, race, nation and so on. Tillich also uses the distinction between the images, conceptions and names of the divine and this category of fundamental anthropology, ultimate concern, to answer the Marxist criticism of religion. The images and conceptions of God are certainly human projections, but the screen which invites and receives the projections is not a projection. It is 'the experienced ultimacy of being and meaning. It is the realm of ultimate concern.'[65] Ernst Bloch took over this argument from Tillich in order to give the Marxist critique a religious rather than an irreligious form.[66] But Tillich's formulation only expresses the idea of God anthropologically, and in anthropology only transcendentally. The 'question of God' arises out of man's experience of himself. This is the experience of his finitude. According to Tillich, finitude is experienced in the threat posed to human existence by non-being and nothingness itself. The question which arises from this is the question of a Being which is superior to this non-being and can overcome it, which by overcoming anxiety can give men and women 'courage to be' in spite of non-being. Only infinite, not finite, being can establish this courage to be in men and women. So Tillich's concept of religion is an 'existential concept of religion'.[67]

Being human is a transcendental 'question mark'. Neverthe-less the infinite being of humankind can only be mediated in the form of finitude, and 'what concerns us ultimately' only in conditioned manifestations and symbols. The inner 'self-transcendence' which Tillich formulates in the same words as Rahner[68] is matched by the manifestation of infinite Being in finitude; indeed this human self-transcendence is itself already a manifestation of Being itself, for the indissoluble connection between all that is finite and Being itself is shown in the infinite striving of finite being.[69] Because Tillich interprets threatened and transcendent human finitude by the psychological concept of 'anxiety', on the other hand he can designate finite being grounded in Being itself as 'ontological courage to be', in order to make the act of faith in God and trust in God anthropolog-ically comprehensible to everyone.

Tillich interprets the specific Christian message on the basis of the presuppositions indicated above: that God has revealed himself in Jesus Christ means the creation of a new being under the conditions of human existence alienated from its origin. Jesus as the bearer of the new being is subject to the conditions of finiture, anxiety, tragedy, conflict and death, 'but he victori-ously maintains unity with God; he sacrifices what is only Jesus in him for what makes him Christ'.[70] In so doing he creates the new being, of which the church is the historical embodiment. Therefore the object of unconditional concern is not the church itself, but the one to whom the church bears witness. It bears witness to him with an existential claim, i.e. as the 'courage to be' everywhere and at all times.

The abolition of the division between sacred and profane in culture follows from the existential concept of religion. Religion is a dimension in all culture. If religion is unconditional concern, then it is no less than the 'substance which gives meaning to culture, and culture is the totality of forms in which the basic concern of religion finds expression'.[71] Culture is the form of religion, and the church has to bear witness to this, but not keep religion to itself. For Tillich, the body of faith is not the church, but culture. Here he follows liberal Protestantism as it was represented by R.Rothe in the nineteenth century and develops his theory of the 'latent church' in order to prove this thesis; Rahner took it over in his own way in his theory of 'anonymous Christians'. The existential concept of religion respects the church's concept of religion, but it transcends it, since it recognizes the fact that outside the church there are many artistic and prophetic forms in which culture expresses ultimate concern. Those who do this are the 'members of the latent church'. They must be recognized by the members of the 'manifest church'. The 'manifest church' must reckon with the existence of the 'latent church' in culture, listen to its criticism, take over its inspiration and criticize its errors. In this connection Tillich says that 'the church did not hear the prophetic voice in Communism and did not recognize its demonic possibilities'.[72] With the help of this theory of the 'latent church' in culture outside the manifest church Tillich, like Rahner after him, tries to universalize the special concern of Christianity. At root, however, even from the start he had related religion less to the church than to culture. Art has a depth-dimension, and modern technology and civilization have the same depth-dimension. Even in modern culture, religion is not an alien body and a relic of the past, but a living expression of 'what ultimately concerns us' and thus the hidden foundation even of modern culture, though this is often denied.

How can that be proved? Tillich sees the dominant idea of modern culture in the domination of nature. The power of science and technology keep expanding. However, as a result of their fascination with it modern men and women have the 'depth-dimension'. Their reality has lost its 'inner transparency to eternity'. At the same time the experiences of human finitude – anxiety, guilt, tragedy and death – were displaced from modern culture. Scientific technological progress became the idol of the modern world. Nevertheless, existential protests have been made since the beginning of industrial society. Neither church conservatism nor enlightened liberalism, but existentialism understood in the widest sense of the word became the religious protest against the spirit of industrial society in the midst of industrial society itself. This existentialist counter-culture in industrial culture is taken up by authentic theology of culture and interpreted as the human situation, so that the message of Christ, the new being, can be related to this human situation. This example clearly shows Tillich's method of the theology of culture; existential analysis penetrates the superficial questions of the day to the existential questions which arise out of the experience of human finitude. It is usually done by the representatives of the 'latent church', by the true and creative people outside the church. The theology of culture takes it up and makes it more profound, in order to relate the Christian message of the 'new being' to the situation of men and women in modern culture. The theology of the church must be open to such a theology of culture, and the 'manifest church' must recognize this 'latent church' in culture. Only then can the manifest church openly put forward the absolute claim of God, or 'what concerns us ultimately', without making itself an absolute. Only then can the church reveal the true theonomy of culture without getting entangled in the helpless efforts of a clerical heteronomy or retreating from the autonomy of culture which is asserted in modern times. Theonomous culture is a culture which is determined by the divine spirit and directed towards it: the divine spirit is the fulfilment of the human spirit.[73]

Tillich's programme of a theology of culture grounded in the church and with a universal responsibility is most fascinating. But he limits his analysis of the situation to an analysis of the existential human situation. Therefore any analysis arrives at

84

the same result. Every human situation is intrinsically the same in its 'depth-dimension', regardless of whether the analysis is of modern culture, mediaeval culture or stone-age culture. In 'what concerns us ultimately', each human existence is confronted with the eternal question of 'being or non-being'. For Tillich, the temporal situation to which he seeks to communicate the Christian message is none other than the situation of human temporality, which however is timeless and does not change. Human finitude threatened by nothingness does not alter its nature in time. Tillich's relevance to the present is only apparent, for his metaphysical theology holds for all times and his method of correlation communicates only what is always there: Being itself and finite being.

Nevertheless, Tillich's mediation between faith and the experience of divine grace and justification must be regarded as successful. For him 'faith' is not a dogmatic conviction or a religious feeling, but is a matter of the whole person being 'grasped' by 'what concerns us ultimately'.[74] And because the experience of the threat of non-being is there, this being grasped leads to a new 'courage to be'.[75] Tillich introduces the concept of 'courage' to describe faith in order to stress that faith is a wager and to stress the dimension of the affirmation of life in faith: faith is the courage for self-affirmation despite the powers of non-being. The courage of faith does not deny that doubts are there, but it affirms them as the expression of finitude, because it affirms unconditional concern despite doubt. Now that is only possible if the believer has that experience of God which was once described as grace or the justification of the sinner. Tillich takes over a category from psychoanalysis and calls it the experience of 'acceptance'.[76] The fact that individuals experience that they are 'accepted' by God despite their doubt and unacceptable qualities is grace. That they can thereafter accept, affirm and love themselves is faith. Therefore Tillich formulates this experience as 'acceptance of self despite all that is unacceptable about us, because we are accepted by God'. Such an experience of faith overcomes not only our human tendency to get above ourselves but also human self-hatred, and means that this does not have to be repressed in the subconscious. It has therapeutic power.

That is particularly significant for men and women of the modern world. The more this world becomes the human world, the more – as I said – men and women become questions which they can no longer answer. The modern loss of self is reflected in mass depressions and in the compulsion to confirm oneself by work and achievement. Tillich's acute analysis has identified this inner problem of modern men and women. But he can only communicate 'justification by grace through faith alone' by means of inward personal experience, and not also to the world which produces such experience among the people who live in it. According to the traditions of the Bible, however, only a new world which is righteous because it has been made righteous accords with the God who is the Creator and the righteous one. Those who have been justified, accepted in grace and inspired with courage for new being can only understand themselves the beginning of this new righteous world. The social, political and cosmic dimensions of righteousness and the kingdom of God do, however, retreat in Tillich's mediating theology behind the stress on human personality. Like Bultmann and Rahner, he takes over the modern human experience of subjectivity and from the Christian tradition communicates primarily the content of personal faith as related to the subject. He does not question the social conditions and the political limitations of this modern experience of subjectivity. The Christian tradition which has been handed down fits without deletions and contradictions into the 'bourgeois religion' of the modern world and its banal principle: 'Religion is a private concern.'

86

4. Political theology and imperfect modernity

Belief in progress in the modern world of Europe and America shattered in the terror of the two twentieth-century world wars. Only the revolutionary socialist movements continued it. However, in the Western world, Fascist dictatorships arose against them. Not only belief in God but human self-confidence itself was lost in the abominations of Auschwitz and Hiroshima. 'God is dead' had been the expression of nineteenth-century atheism. 'Man is dead' became the expression of twentieth-century nihilism. This internal spiritual collapse of the bourgeois Christian world was matched by the external, political collapse of the European colonial empires and the liberation of the oppressed and exploited peoples of Latin America, Africa and Asia. That internal collapse was also matched by the so-far unstoppable spread of the ecological crisis: the exploitation and destruction of nature on earth by industry. The optimism for the future which had mobilized scientific technological civilization turned to catastrophic fatalism in the face of the irreparable devastation which it had brought about. In a situation of such ambivalence in modernity it is not helpful to relate the Christian message only to the liberated subjectivity of modern men and women, as Bultmann, Rahner, Tillich and many other modern theologians have done so impressively. One must get to the foundations and aims of this risky project that is the modern world, for these foundations and aims have themselves become so questionable that humankind cannot survive without a change in its aims and methods. Within the bounds of the 'bourgeois religion' of this society which has become so dangerous, Christianity at any rate has no chance of unfolding the critical, liberating and healing powers of its message.

In the twentieth century the churches and many Christians have had to experience conflict, resistance and persecution to a degree greater than in almost any earlier century of their history. The suppression of the churches under the socialism of the USSR, the church struggle under Fascism, the persecution of Christians in Latin-American dictatorships have dissolved the old syntheses of church and state and the old symbioses of Christianity and culture. These modern experiences of Christian faith call for another 'mediating theology', a theology which communicates the Christian message not only through adaptation but also through confrontation, and looks not only for correspondences but also for the necessary conflicts. Political theology[77] became the starting point for a whole series of mediating theologies of this kind: the theology of revolution, the theology of liberation, black theology, feminist theology and other regionally conditioned, 'contextual' theologies in Africa and Asia. One of its theological foundations can be found in the 'theology of hope', which mediates between eschatological redemption and historical liberations.[78]

1. It is amazing that of the four basic philosophical questions which Kant formulated he addressed the question 'What may I hope for?' to religion. Up to that point religion had always been directed towards the eternal and based on tradition. But with the beginning of modernity, the future came into the centre of the human spirit. The religious question becomes the question of hope, of personal, social and universal hope. The modern mind no longer experiences the world as a natural world enclosed in itself, but as world history open to the future, open to salvation and danger. If the world is comprehended in history, then only the future decides its fate. People anticipate this future in their minds with fear and hope. They seek hope in danger. Therefore 'the future' has become the modern paradigm for transcendence. When in the nineteenth century people still felt certain that they knew who man was and therefore declared man to be the measure of all things, there

88

came into being the anthropological criticism of religion as put forward by Feuerbach, Marx, Freud and Nietzsche. But now that men and women today have become uncertain of themselves and monstrous, they can only look for a disclosure of their true being from the future of a new world situation which will become the 'homeland of their identity'. Therefore they no longer relate the traditions of the past only to their present situation but also to their future and the future of the world, and seek hopes in their recollections and therefore future in the past. The old anthropological criticism and legacy of religion is then replaced by an eschatology of religion looking towards the consummation of the world, which sets free that hope which is vested in religious traditions and symbols.

The biblical traditions are particularly open to this perspective, because they form the foundation of the 'Abrahamite religions': Judaism, Christianity and Islam. These Abrahamite religions are religions of hope and exodus. At their origin stands no mythical primal event, but the exodus of Abraham on the basis of the promise of the God who is as yet unknown to him. Israel came into being out of an analogous basic experience of exodus from slavery in Egypt, under the leadership of Moses, on the basis of the divine promise. Christianity came into being out of Jesus' liberating message of the imminent kingdom of God and the apostles' liberating message of the resurrection of the crucified Christ to eternal life. In essence Israel and the church of Christ are to be termed bearers of hope and therefore messianic religions. In them the messianic tenor of all religions is manifest: 'Where there is hope there is religion.'[79] They manifest the messianic character of the historical liberations of oppressed and suffering humankind. Therefore Kant acutely put to these religions the unusual question 'What may I hope for?' and expected an answer from them to the terrors of history.

2. The second basic question which modernity has raised for

traditional belief in God is in theory the problem of theodicy and in practice the unbounded dismay at 'Auschwitz' and the terrible fear of the mass murder of men and women in a nuclear war which is possible at any time. In the nineteenth century protest-atheism responded, wrongly, to the experience of suffering by denying God: 'Wash away every cause of suffering in life, and you can prove that God exists. Listen, philosopher – why do I suffer? That is the rock of atheism. The least little twinge of pain tears a hole in God's creation from top to bottom,' wrote the revolutionary German Poet Georg Büchner at that time in *Danton's Death*, in words which he put into the mouth of Tom Paine.[80] By contrast the incomparably more cruel experiences of the twentieth century have led to a new kind of protest-theism, i.e. a longing for God on the basis of the hunger for justice in the world: 'Theology... is the hope that this injustice by which the world is characterized is not permanent, that injustice may not be the last word. It is the expression of a longing that the murderer may not triumph over his innocent victim,' wrote Max Horkheimer, founder of 'critical theory' in the 'Frankfurt school', in 1970.[81] Therefore for many people today the question is not so much the atheistic question whether one can still talk of God 'after Auschwitz', but the quite new theistic question of whom one can talk after 'Auschwitz', if not of God. For them 'God' becomes a word for the transcendental, unconditional and all-determining protest against Auschwitz, against Hiroshima and against the threat of human self-annihilation. In this respect a new theology has come into being today, of the cross, of the suffering God, of the pain and the love of God, which recognizes Golgotha in the 'sufferings of this time' and the sufferings of this time in Golgotha.[82]

3. The 'ecological crisis', the increasing destruction of the natural environment, the growing annihilation of species of plants and animals, and the exploitation of the non-renewable resources of the earth now shows clearly the self-contradictory

nature of the project of modernity, of 'scientific technological civilization'.[83] This is no longer just a crisis in the exhausted natural environment of human culture which could be overcome by technological means but a crisis in the life-system of the modern world itself. Nature is being subjected and exploited by human technology. The modern sciences provide the knowledge which enables us to subject nature. The basic values of modern society which have produced these sciences and technologies are the will to power, progress in accumulating power and the safeguarding of power. Even if 'belief' in progress has been lost, modern industrial society continues to be programmed for power, growth and progress. The old values of pre-industrial society like equilibrium, compensation, harmony and making human culture at home in self-regenerating nature have been displaced. But as a result 'progress' is steering modern, scientific technological civilization with fatal certainty into increasingly great environmental catastrophes and ultimately to the universal, ecological death of all life on earth. The essential religious basis of modern expansion and gaining power over nature was and is a misunderstood form of Jewish-Christian religion with its first divine command to man: 'Subdue the earth' (Gen.1.28).[84] In the late Middle Ages and the time of the Renaissance people began to wonder at and worship God predominantly as the 'almighty'. It was not his goodness but his overwhelming power which became the prime characteristic of his divinity. If God, 'the Almighty', is lord and master of the world, then man as his 'image' on earth must do all he can to become lord and master of nature, for only by seizing power over the earth can man accord with his God. Whereas hitherto in the West nature had been respected as the 'mother of all living things', now it was degraded to being the slave of humankind, and handed over as 'ownerless property' to the first person to master it.[85]

The change of direction needed from the fatal danger which

the modern world has brought upon itself must therefore be a change in its essential religious foundations. According to the biblical tradition, God, to be in whose image is the supreme value of humankind, is not 'omnipotence', but in his being and his existence 'love' (I John 4.16). Men and women accord with God, not in seizing power over nature but through a communion with it which is shaped by loving 'reverence for life' (A.Schweitzer). It follows from this that human beings can claim the right to use nature but not to dispose of it. At a time of systematic disposing of nature, faith in nature as God's creation must lead to conflict with and resistance to its exploitation and destruction by human beings. Christian creation-faith is now alive in the cultural resistance movement of ecological groups and is lived out credibly by them.

4. Not least, attention should be paid to a major change in the criterion of truth in the modern world. From of old, truth was understood as correspondence and accord: for a concept to correspond with the matter to which it related was regarded as its truth (*adaequatio rei et intellectus*). The correspondence between the laws of human society and the laws of the natural world was taken to show the rightness of these laws. The correspondence between human nature and the eternal divine nature from which it arose was regarded as the truth and justification of human existence. 'Truth' was understood as equilibrium, correspondence and peace. With the beginning of modernity in Europe this criterion of truth changed fundamentally. Now praxis became the criterion of truth, human praxis in the widest sense of the word, which includes moral praxis as well as technical praxis: the historical praxis of human beings. Kant already said that everything in the religious tradition which had no practical implications was dogmatism and superstition. For faith in modern times he would only allow 'what it is possible and useful to accept in a practical (moral) sense'.[86] Accordingly human reason acknowledges in

92

nature only 'that which it has itself put into nature'.[87] This thoroughgoing orientation on praxis has led to the instrumentalizing of human reason. Reason is no longer an organ of perception but an operative, planning human organ. The rational is no longer seen as the theoretical correspondence between knowledge and that which is known, but as the effectiveness of the relationship between means and ends in practice. The modern critique of religion no longer makes any critique of the content of faith, but is a purely functional critique of the psychological, political and social effects of this faith. It no longer asks whether it is true or false, but only whether it has the function of oppression or liberation, alienation or humanization. In this way, it too makes praxis the criterion of the truth of religion. Under these conditions it is necessary for theology self-critically to accept praxis as the criterion of truth and no longer to stress just the orthodoxy of faith but also the orthopraxy of love. Both theological and personal and political praxis are involved in a dialectical relationship. Critical theology reflects on praxis in the light of the gospel and realizes it in new praxis.[88] Praxis itself takes on cognitive relevance. This is the starting point of the new political theology: 'The philosophers have only interpreted the world in various ways; the point, however, is to change it' (Marx, 'Eleventh Thesis on Feuerbach'). A theology of hope for the kingdom of God which changes the world leads to a historical awareness of change. Through criticism of the previous praxis of Christians and churches in modern society and through the anticipation of the hoped-for new creation of all things, it becomes topical.[89]

But the more Christian theology in this way accepts praxis as the criterion of truth, the more it will also perceive its limitations. The operationalization of human reason has certainly made this more effective, but it has also made it poorer. The old forms of meditative and total perception of things and living beings has become alien to modern men and

93

women. Many of them feel this impoverishment personally. The methods of purely analytical science exhaust themselves. The orientation on praxis has led more recent political theology at a very early stage to an appreciation and acceptance of mystical experience.[90] The practical political relationship to truth under the slogan of 'realization' calls for an expansion through a relationship to truth in meditation and mysticism, in the experience of accord, correspondence and peace.

I have outlined four problem areas in which the scientific technological project of the modern world has found itself in contradictions. Christian theology has the task of relating the Christian tradition and message critically and therapeutically to this modern situation, for only in that way can it communicate the tradition of Christian faith, love and hope. This 'mediation' calls for both adaptation and contradiction. Theology must accept the changed circumstances of the world in order to change these in its turn towards peace, justice and the life of creation.

Notes

1. P.Tillich, 'Die technische Stadt als Symbol', in *Die religiöse Substanz der Kultur. Schriften zur Theologie der Kultur*, Gesammelte Werke IX, Stuttgart 1967, 309f. (italics).

2. J.-P.Sartre, *Existentialism and Humanism*, London 1948, 33f.

3. H.J.Kraus, *Geschichte der historisch-kritischen Erforschung des Alten Testaments*, Neukirchen-Vluyn ³1982.

4. Cf. A.Schweitzer, *The Quest of the Historical Jesus*, London and New York (1910) ³1954.

5. E.Troeltsch, *The Absoluteness of Christianity and the History of Religion*, Richmond, Va. 1971 and London 1972, 85ff.; id., *Der Historismus und seine Überwindung*, Berlin 1924, 3ff.

6. G.E.Lessing, *On the Proof of the Spirit and of Power*, in *Lessing's Theological Writings*, ed. H.Chadwick, London 1956, 55.

7. W.Dilthey, *Gesammelte Schriften* VIII, Stuttgart ³1962, 225.

8. W.Herrmann, *The Communion of the Christian with God. Described on the Basis of Luther's Statements* (1896), ET Philadelphia and London 1972, 76.

9. D.F.Strauss, *Die christliche Glaubenslehre* I, Stuttgart 1840 (reprinted Darmstadt 1973), 71; cf. also F.Nietzsche, 'The Use and Abuse of History', in *Thoughts out of Season*, London 1909, II, 1–100.

10. E.Troeltsch, *The Absoluteness of Christianity*, 90.

11. F.Schleiermacher, *The Christian Faith*, Edinburgh 1928, esp. §§ 93-112.

12. W.Herrmann, *Ethik*, Tübingen ⁵1913.

13. W.Herrmann, 'Gottes Offenbarung an uns' (1908), in *Schriften zur Grundlegung der Theologie* II, ed. P.Fischer-Appelt, TB 36/II, Munich 1967, 155.

14. Cf. e.g. K.Jaspers, 'Einleitung in die Philosophie', in *Philosophie I: Philosophische Weltorientierung*, Berlin 1932, 15ff.

15. W.Herrmann, 'Die Auffassung der Religion in Cohens und Natorps Ethik' (1909), in *Schriften zur Grundlegung der Theologie* II, 228f.

16. R.Bultmann, *Glauben und Verstehen*, I-IV, Tübingen 1933-1965 (English translations of I, *Faith and Understanding*, London and New York 1969; II, *Essays Philosophical and Theological*, London 1955).

17. R.Bultmann, 'Religion und Kultur' (1920), in *Anfänge der dialektischen Theologie*, ed. J.Moltmann, II, Munich 1963, 1920 (partly italic in the original).

18. Ibid., 23.

19. Cf. R.Bultmann, *Faith and Understanding*, 55f.

20. Cf. R.Bultmann, *Essays*, 292; cf. also *Theology of the New Testament*, London and New York 1952, 196.

21. R.Bultmann, 'New Testament and Mythology' (1941), in *New Testament and Mythology and other basic writings*, Philadelphia and London 1985, 1-44; 'The Problem of Hermeneutics', in *Essays*, 234-61; cf. H.W.Bartsch (ed.), *Kerygma und Mythos* I-IV, Hamburg 1948ff. (partial ET in *Kerygma and Myth*, *Kerygma and Myth 2*, London 1953, 1962).

22. Cf. R.Bultmann, 'Das Problem einer theologischen Exegese des Neuen Testaments' (1925), in *Anfänge der dialektischen Theologie* II, 47-72.

23. R.Bultmann, *History and Eschatology*, Edinburgh 1957, 153.

24. R.Bultmann, 'New Testament and Mythology', 4.

25. Ibid., 8, 12f.

26. C.F.von Weizsäcker, *Die Einheit der Natur*, Munich 1971; W.Heisenberg, *The Physicist's Conception of Nature*, London 1958.

27. J.Moltmann, 'Existenzgeschichte und Weltgeschichte. Auf dem Wege zu einer politischen Hermeneutik des Evangeliums', in *Perspektiven der Theologie. Gesammelte Aufsätze*, Munich 1968, 128-48; J.B.Metz, *Theology of the World*, London and New York 1969.

28. F.Belo, *A Materialist Reading of the Gospel of Mark*, Maryknoll 1981.

29. R.Descartes, *Discourse on Method* (1692), London (Everyman, nd), 49.

30. Cf.M.Heidegger, 'Die Zeit des Weltbildes', in *Holzwege*, Frankfurt ³1957, 69-104.

31. M.Buber, *The Way of Man*, London 1950.

32. I.Kant, *On Logic*, Introduction, London 1957, 29.

33. M.Heidegger, *Kant und das Problem der Metaphysik*, Bonn 1929, 193ff.

34. Cf.P.Melanchthon, *Loci Communes* (1521) and the form of questions in the (Reformed) Heidelberg Catechism (1563).

35. L.Feuerbach, *Vorlesungen über das Wesen der Religion*, in L.Feuerbachs Sämmtliche Werke, ed. W.Bolin and F.Jodl, Vol.8, Stuttgart 1908.

36. Karl Marx, *Early Writings*, Harmondsworth 1975, 244, 251.

37. Thus K.P.Fischer, *Der Mensch als Geheimnis. Die Anthropologie Karl Rahners*, Freiburg, Basel and Vienna 1974, 296.

38. His main works are *Theological Investigations* (20 volumes), London and New York 1961ff.; *Foundations of Christian Faith*, London and New York 1978.

39. Karl Rahner, 'Transcendentaltheologie', in *Sacramentum Mundi. Theologisches Lexikon für die Praxis* IV, Freiburg, Basel and Vienna 1969, col.987.

40. *Theological Investigations* 11, 1974, 100.

41. K.P.Fischer, *Der Mensch als Geheimnis*, 227.

42. *Theological Investigations* 6, 1969, 390-8.

43. *Theological Investigations* 6, 392.

44. *Theological Investigations* 5, 1966, 107.

45. *Theological Investigations* 5, 110.

46. *Theological Investigations* 6, 394.

47. Ibid.

48. Ibid.

49. *Theological Investigations* 1, 1961, 197.

50. *Theological Investigations* 1, 186.

51. *Theological Investigations* 1, 164 n.1.

52. *Theological Investigations* 3, 1967, 28.

53. *Theological Investigations* 1, 172.

54. *Theological Investigations* 5, 1966, 165.

55. *Cf. Theological Investigations*, 5, 172.

56. J.Moltmann, 'Christsein, Menschsein und das Reich Gottes', *Stimmen der Zeit* 203.9, 1985, 619-31.

57. P.Tillich, *Die religiöse Substanz der Kultur. Schriften zur Theologie der Kultur*, Gesammelte Werke IX, Stuttgart 1967.

I am not going into Tillich's early *socialist* phase here, but limiting myself to his late *metaphysical* phase, which developed after his emigration from Germany to the USA necessitated by his political resistance. It took classic form in his *Systematic Theology*, through which it became influential.

58. Cf. *Systematic Theology* I, Chicago and Welwyn Garden City 1951, reissued London 1978, 3.

59. Ibid., 6.

60. Ibid., 61.

61. Ibid., 61f.

62. Ibid., 12.

63. Ibid.

64. *Bekenntnisschriften der Evangelisch-Lutherischen Kirche*, Göttingen 1952, 560.

65. P.Tillich, *Systematic Theology* I, 212.

66. Cf. E.Bloch, *Das Prinzip Hoffnung*, 1529, ET *The Principle of Hope*, Oxford 1986.

67. P.Tillich, *Systematic Theology* I, 214.

68. Cf. ibid., 186ff.

69. Cf. ibid., 188.

70. *Die religiöse Substanz der Kultur*, 100.

71. Ibid., 101.

72. Ibid., 109.

73. Cf. ibid., 82-93.

74. *Wesen und Wandel des Glaubens*, Weltperspektiven vol.8, Berlin 1961, 9.

75. *The Courage to Be*, New York and Welwyn Garden City 1952.

76. P.Tillich, *Systematic Theology* III, Chicago and Welwyn Garden City 1964, reissued London 1978, 224ff.

77. German discussions are J.B.Metz, *Theology of the World*, London and New York 1969; D.Sölle, *Politische Theologie. Auseinandersetzung mit Rudolf Bultmann*, Stuttgart (1971) 1982; J.Moltmann, *Politische Theologie – Politische Ethik*, Munich (1971) 1983.

78. J.Moltmann, *Theology of Hope*, London and New York 1967.

79. E.Bloch, *Das Prinzip Hoffnung*, 1404.

80. G.Büchner, *Danton's Death*, Act 3, Scene 13, London 1968, 57.

81. M.Horkheimer, *Die Sehnsucht nach dem ganz Anderen*, Hamburg 1970, 61f.

82. K.Kitamori, *Theology of the Pain of God*, Richmond, Va. and London 1964; J.Moltmann, *The Crucified God*, London and New York 1974; E.Jüngel, *God as the Mystery of the World*, Grand Rapids and Edinburgh 1983.

83. A.Peccei, *Die Zukunft in unserer Hand. Gedanken und Reflexionen des Präsidenten des Club of Rome*, Vienna 1981; see also the studies by the Club of Rome: *The Limits of Growth*, New York 1972; *The Global 2000 Report to the President*, edited by the Council on Environmental Quality, Washington 1980.

84. Cf. J.Moltmann, *God in Creation, An ecological doctrine of creation*, London and San Francisco 1985, II.1, 'The Crisis of Domination', 23ff.

85. W.Leiss, *The Domination of Nature*, New York 1972.

86. I.Kant, *Streit der Fakultäten* (1798), PhB 252, Hamburg 1959, 37.

87. I.Kant, Preface to the second edition of the *Critique of Pure Reason*, ed. Noel Kemp Smith, London [2]1933, 20.

88. Cf. G.Gutiérrez, *Theology of Liberation*, Maryknoll 1973 and London 1974, 6ff.

89. This method has come to be adopted at ecumenical conferences and meetings, especially in the Third World.

90. J.B.Metz, *Zeit der Orden? Zur Mystik und Politik der Nachfolge*, Freiburg 1977; J.Moltmann, *Experiences of God*, London and Philadelphia 1980: D.Sölle, *Die Hinreise. Zur religiösen Erfahrung*, Stuttgart ³1976.